TABLE OF C

Layered Curriculum:

The practical solution for teachers with more than one student in their classroom

2nd edition

Kathie F. Nunley

ISBN 1-929358-12-1

Additional copies of this book as well as all books by
Kathie F. Nunley are available at:
http://Help4Teachers.com
or Email: Kathie@brains.org

Cover Design by Micheal R. Eudy
Eudy Animation   Dallas, Texas

published by
BRAINS.ORG
Amherst, NH
books@brains.org

Printed in the USA by Morris Publishing
Kearney, NE 68847

Acknowledgments

So many people have assisted me in the writing of this book. I again must thank my wonderfully supportive husband and patient children. And a big thanks to my colleagues and fellow teachers who have been so willing to share their thoughts, opinions, and creative minds.

This book is dedicated to my mother.

Like teaching, mothering is often a thankless job. When we are young, we do not recognize the need to say thank you. When we are old enough, we seldom take the time to go back.

The suspense is terrible. . . I hope it will last. - Willy Wonka.

Chapter One

Santa Don't Come to the Projects

Teaching is one of the great joys of life. Our interaction with young people is an experience like no other. I think it is what calls us back to the classroom each year.

For each year is a new beginning, a renewed opportunity to touch the future through young minds. But with the power that lies in our position comes a great responsibility. There must be constant reflection on our methods and philosophies. For although we strive to make a difference and improve the lives of the children, above all else, we should do no harm.

I love to teach. Teaching is an art which takes advantage of creativity. My views on education, philosophies of instruction, and teaching methods have been evolving with every school year. Life events both in and out of school create the lens through which I view this profession.

✧

My teaching career began in the inner-city schools of a low socioeconomic region in the south. Teaching to this 98% African-American low SES population made for some creative opportunities.

These are schools where every teacher used an overhead projector so that you never turned your back on the class. Thus, I was introduced to teaching in a highly secured facility.

I was particularly influenced by an experience I had teaching a pilot program for illiterate males repeating science for the third time. These "repeated failures" as they were classified, were a fascinating bunch who eventually referred to themselves as the "Nunley Boys". This group of children, ranging in age from 15 to 18, were the equivalent to the *sweat hogs* of our community. Disliked, feared and basically unloved, this group comprised my fourth period general biology class. Other teachers would ask me if I was frightened to have all these boys together in one class. I would chuckle and shake my head at their ignorance. What they didn't understand or know was the safety and love shared by this special population.

One of the first eye-openers came near Thanksgiving when the topic of Santa Claus came up. One of the students piped up with "Ms. Nunley, don't you know Santa don't come to the Projects?"

"What do you mean, Santa doesn't come?" I naively asked.

They then began to tell me the stories that their mothers and grandmothers had given for why Santa didn't come to their homes on Christmas eve. Until that moment I had never thought what it must be like to raise a child in this culture where Santa is seen everywhere and promises to bring things, but on Christmas morning, the story brings nothing but disappointment.

"My mother told me 'Santa is too scared to come to the Projects.'"

"Grandma told me 'Santa's sleigh got hit by a plane'".

"When I was eight years old, I asked Santa for a bike and he said he'd bring it, so I told all my friends I was gettin' a bike. They didn't believe me, but I kept sayin', 'yep, Santa told me'. Then on Christmas morning, I looked, but no bike. All my friends say, 'so where's your new bike?' I just said, 'Oh, it's at my grandma's' or 'Oh, my brother's ridin it' or make up somethin' til they quit askin".

By the end of the period, I was fighting back tears.

The next day, we made Christmas stockings. I had construction paper, glitter, glue, string, etc. and they had to make a stocking - no arguments. I told them it was an assignment and they had to decorate it with the various kingdoms of life. They grumbled and groaned, but they each made a stocking which we hung in the chalk tray at the front of the room. I told them that Santa might not come to the Housing Projects, but he did sometimes come to schools.

Everyday, there was something in their stockings. It wasn't much, maybe just a home-made cookie or a little candy sucker, but something was there. Then a funny thing started to happen. The boys started coming up with excuses to come in to the classroom early in the morning.

Karl might wander in with "Ms. Nunley, mind if I leave my backpack in here til class?"

"Sure", I'd say, "that's fine".

So Karl would saunter in. You have to picture this big, tall, gang member who lives on the street as often as in a home, coming in with the appropriate machismo bounce in his walk, tossing the backpack behind my desk, then muttering, " Well, 'long as I'm here, might as well check the stocking". In a little while here would come another one, with his excuse for entering the room and checking his stocking.

Sometimes these boys would show up with cuts and bumps because they knew I had a first-aid kit and would help them clean it and bandage it. Sometimes they'd come in for a peanut butter sandwich in the morning because they knew there was always bread and peanut butter in the cabinet.

One day Bobby came from his cooking class with something wrapped in foil which he tossed on my desk.

"Is this for me?" I asked.

"Yeah, whatever," he mumbled, looking at his shoes. Then, "Oh, man, I almost forgot" as he reached into his back pocket for the fork which he set by the foil.

He had made me a pizza. It was the worst looking piece of pizza you had ever seen in your life, but you better believe I ate it all, with delight.

Going to "the outside"

As it was a biology class, we frequently talked about state parks and areas surrounding our city. One day I jokingly mentioned that if they all passed the course that semester, we'd all go on a camping trip to a state park just across the state line, "the outside" as they called it. Well, you guessed it, they all passed and they held me to my promise. After a discussion with my principal, we decided that a week-end camping trip to the park would be feasible with some help from the community. The local newspaper came out and did a story, took a picture of the class and everything. Those boys were so thrilled to see themselves on the front page for something non-criminal. We got a few calls from people horrified that my principal would as one caller put it, "let some white woman go off into the woods with a bunch of black boys!" But most calls were supportive and the donations came flooding in. We had tents, sleeping bags and enough food for an army. The trip was a success. Several other teachers (male and female) volunteered to come along. The rules were simple - no guns, no drugs. The boys understood. We roasted marshmallows, rented canoes, pitched tents and listened to bird calls. The boys were on *the outside*.

You must build a relationship of trust before you can have a teaching-learning relationship. Few, if any of these children had stable homes. Most had criminal records, some serious. I visited with more of their parol officers than parents. People feared them. They were unloved. And that - was their greatest problem. That was the year that I learned first hand that every child needed to be loved. A kind word, a safe place, a peanut butter sandwich when you're hungry. These are basic needs.

So when those other teachers inquired with whispers in the hallway, "Aren't you scared to death to have all those boys in one room?" I knew the real answer was that it was the safest place on earth. Those boys would never harm me. In fact, they would kill for me (I'm afraid that may be literally). I still wonder about those boys, Karl, Bobby, Duck, Clarence and the others, and miss them terribly. I hope I taught them half as much as they taught me.

Every Child Deserves a Special Education

In addition to my teaching and research, I am also the mother of four children. While I am a regular education teacher, I am a special education parent. My oldest child is my 20 year old son, Keegan. Keegan has autism. Although he has what is termed very high-functioning autism, raising Keegan has probably been the single most important influence on my educational philosophies. From Keegan I have learned not to take learning for granted. What many of us learn through everyday modeling, some have to learn through direct instruction. From Keegan I have also learned the importance of letting all students have an equal chance to learn. No one wants to feel singled out or special due to a disability. He has also taught me to never underestimate the potential of special education students.

I also have a beautiful 16 year old daughter. In addition to teaching me important points about teen heartthrobs and music, I have learned from her about brain plasticity. She has been recovering from a depressed skull fracture since her first birthday. A head-on collision with a drunk driver resulted in damage to the frontal lobes of her brain and an immediate loss in her speech and hearing.

Watching her recovery from the brain-damage has taught me a great deal about the brain's ability to accommodate, rearrange and redesign. This ability is known as brain plasticity.

When the damage to her brain resulted in her losing both her speech and her hearing, we were forced to start her in public education at the age of 13 months. The infant stimulation program was incredibly effective and today my daughter speaks and hears like any other 16 year old. Since the parts of her brain responsible for speaking and hearing were damaged, other areas were trained to perform those functions. The recovery was so successful that today she attends a school for gifted and talented students.

I also have a ten year old son, who was our first child to enter into "regular education" - a real eye opener for my husband who was very nervous that there is no IEP and shocked to discover one has to take "pot-luck" when it comes to classes, teachers and instruction. It was hard to explain to him why every student is not entitled to a special education. Needless to say my husband breathed a sigh of relief last year when this son was diagnosed with dyslexia - so here we go again.

Last, but not least is my seven year old son, who, as any parent of a seven year old can tell you, should probably be in classified as a special education student for no other reason than he's seven! Actually he is especially delightful for me to watch at this juncture in my life as I now have a stronger background in brain development and I delight in watching his neurons bloom with dendrites nearly before my eyes.

Mankind should be our business Ebenezer, but it seldom is.
— Jacob Marlee

Chapter Two

The Evolution of Layered Curriculum

The idea for Layered Curriculum began in the late 1980's when I first took a look at the learning styles work being done primarily with Rita Dunn and her associates. The learning styles movement was the first time that education "came out of the closet" so to speak and openly acknowledged that one size does not fit all. This came at a critical time in education when desegregation and the inclusion mandates from the 1970's had been around long enough to generate a bushel of problems.

America had come to terms with the flagrant discrimination which had occurred in schools. They saw how tracking was too often a smoke screen for segregation, that separate but equal was not necessarily so. Research was showing that students benefitted most from heterogenous classrooms and parents were demanding that segregation for color, disability and language be eliminated.

Teachers were finding that the old stand and deliver methods that had been used in their building for generations were failing. For the first time, teachers were asked to teach to a wide variety of abilities, cultures and languages. If America was truly going to educate the masses, something had to change.

The Learning Styles literature was one of the first serious attempts to help educators address these changes. Teachers began looking at the physical, social and emotional differences and needs of children. Suddenly school boards, professional development planners, teachers and administrators starting looking seriously at issues such as time of day, light, dietary needs, classroom furniture, material and arrangement, and instructional strategies. (Unfortunately, architects were not looking at learning styles during this period and as many of us have seen, and we were left with many new windowless schools. But I digress.)

To get back to my original topic, the evolution of Layered Curriculum, I believe it was conceived and began to take root in my early teaching days as I first started pondering how to address diversity in my classroom. I looked at various learning styles models and they intrigued me. At that point I "played around" with the teaching techniques for a few years and found them quite valuable and necessary.

I was satisfied in my journey toward accommodating learning styles and thought I was being a very accommodating teacher, until another brilliant mind came along and re-directed my thinking. A man by the name of Howard Gardner introduced to me the idea of Multiple Intelligences. Gardner's work pointed out how educators were perhaps spending too much time speaking to the logical and linguistic intelligent child and too little time directed toward children with other strengths, e.g.: the musical or interpersonal intelligences. I looked at Gardner's work too, and realized that it had significant importance to this new and varied classroom.

About the time that I tried to inter-play multiple intelligences with learning styles, I was struck by another voice in education — Anthony Gregorc. Tony Gregorc introduced me to Mind Styles. Gregorc's work illustrated 4 styles of the mind - concrete sequential, concrete random, abstract sequential, abstract random. He was able to graphically show educators the problems encountered when an abstract random minded child finds his way into a concrete sequential minded teacher's classroom. Children who can't function sequentially often find themselves in the vice-principal's office. On the other hand, one also has to feel empathy for the concrete sequential child trying to outline a lecture given by the free thinking abstract random teacher. I looked at Gregorc's work too, and realized its importance in education.

To add more worries to my dilemma was the realization that someone had put special education children in my room. And they just kept coming. The growth in special education has been exponential. *Inclusion, Mainstreaming* and *Least Restrictive Environment* were creeping into the vocabulary of the regular education teacher. The problem was that no one had prepared us for their coming nor told us what to do with them when they arrived.

I suddenly had identified diversity in my students which was staggering. Between Learning Styles, Mind Styles, Multiple Intelligences, various abilities and exceptionalities, multiple languages and cultures, I began to come to two very important conclusions. First, although I am considered a *regular educator* there are no *regular students* in my room. And secondly, *Every student deserves a special education.*

Where are the Regular Students in Regular Education?

Since the 1970's the numbers of students in special education have increased by 400 percent. The numbers are so high, that the ratio is now seven to one. In other words, for every eight children in this country in public education, one is a special education student.

Why the big increase? It's not because people are suddenly giving birth in large numbers to children with disabilities. In fact, the numbers of birth defects have been going down as pre-natal care has gone up. We can find three principle causes for the increase in special education numbers. First, instruments psychologists and school districts use to detect disabilities have become more sophisticated. We are now able to identify disabilities or risk of disability sooner.

Secondly, parents are better informed. They understand what services their children are entitled to and they are organized enough to work the system and get those services. Parent support and advocacy groups are strong, powerful and effective.

Thirdly, and most significantly, we as a nation have become more compassionate. If you look at disabilities as an event on a continuum, you will see that we are all disabled to some extent. It's just a matter of drawing a line somewhere on the continuum and then declaring that everyone on the left is disabled, everyone on the right, is not. As the years go on, we keep moving the line. Basically the emotion of the country asks that we include just a few more, and just a few more, and so on, until the line on the continuum has moved a significant distance and we have a lot more people on the left side of that line than we used to.

This movement reflects itself in the general classroom. The regular education teacher is finding himself faced with increasing diversity and fewer and fewer "regular" students. In fact as I mentioned earlier, it was becoming obvious to many, that there are no "regular" students in regular education.

If we look at a typical classroom of 32 students, we will find four students who have been officially identified by the special education system. These are students who have individualized education plans (IEP's) with written modifications that must be made to their instruction. In some cases the regular classroom teacher has been informed of these modifications, but frequently they have not. Despite federal law which mandates that all people involved in the education of a student be informed of the modifications and have access to the IEP, many schools leave the regular education teacher completely in the dark.

In the same classroom, you have another four students I call the *unidentified special education students*. These are students who should be identified as special education students but are not. These children have either thus far escaped the attention of the special ed department or, as is often the case at the secondary level, these are students who once were in special education, but have dropped out. Often students will go through elementary school in special ed, but once they hit junior or senior high, they don't want the stigma associated with being in special education and have their parent opt them out of the program.

Special education is not the only source of diversity and challenge in the regular classroom. In addition to the special education students, the typical classroom will also have two students with an attention deficit disorder, and two who do not speak English as their native language. Obviously, depending on your community, these numbers may be much higher. For example Attention Deficit Disorder runs in families, so depending on where you teach, you may have a far greater number of ADD or ADHD students in the room.

In this same widely mixed classroom, you are also trying to accommodate a variety of learning styles. The classroom will contain about eight visual learners, seven auditory learners, and about 18 tactile learners who learn best by manipulating material.

The tactile learners are generally the ones who present the greatest challenge to teachers. Designing instructional strategies for tactile learners is difficult for most teachers because that is not our learning style. Teachers, for the most part, are visual and auditory learners, and our preference is to teach in our own personal learning style. We know that teachers are primarily visual and auditory learners because teachers have all successfully completed college. And college screens for the visual and auditory learner.

Individual Modifications

Accommodating the needs of this tremendously diverse group is no small task for the regular education teacher. How do we modify instruction for all these students? In the past, we've been asked to make *individual modifications* based on suggestions by the resource or special education teacher. These may have included things like highlighting important ideas in the textbook, having peer tutors, reducing class and homework assignments for specific students, having a note taker, preferential seating, assistive technology, extended time, alternate tests, and the list goes on and on.

There are several very serious problems with individual modifications. First, and probably least, these individual modifications are tremendously overwhelming to the regular education teacher. In addition to the wide demands put on a teacher in a large diverse classroom population, this additional request was often overlooked or done sporadically at best.

The second, and more significant problem with individual modification is that it is extremely stigmatizing to the student. Regardless of how discreet you may be when you tell a student that he can do fewer homework problems or that she can go down to the resource room for her test, the student knows they have a "special program" as does the rest of the class. The most common reason for students dropping out of special education, particularly at the secondary level, is the stigma attached to special education.

In addition to overwhelming the teacher and stigmatizing the learner, individual modifications have created grading nightmares for the classroom teacher. Teachers do not always know how to handle the grading process in a traditional room and the issue always arises about *fairness*. Is it fair to give the same grade to a student who has been assigned only half the math problems as the student who has done them all?

Third, and most important is that individual modifications discriminate against and deprive other students in the room who would benefit from the same modifications. This is a serious flaw in the system. If I have a student in the room who is a poor reader and needs assignments read to her, there is a very good chance that I have other students in my room who would also benefit from this same modification but are not allowed to have it because he or she has not been identified by the system. This discrepancy became quite obvious to me the year I had a student who had among other things, very "poor executive functioning skills". In other words, he had trouble organizing and planning. His IEP stated that his regular classroom teacher was to check his planner at the end of the day to make sure he had his assignments written down and then verbally go over with him what materials he would need to take home with him in order to complete the assignment. Now I ask you - what parent out there has a child that would not benefit from this! I've never met a parent who at one time or another hasn't been completely frustrated with a child who has come home without materials or with incomplete assignment instructions.

A colleague of mine with a long background in special ed once told me that special education isn't special - it's just effective. I agree, special education is just good education that is tailored to the individual strengths and needs of individual children. And that is when I realized what has come to be my personal mission: ***Every student does indeed deserve a special education.***

Out of this mix of inclusion, stigma, Learning Styles, Multiple Intelligences, Mind Styles and cultural diversity, came the idea for *Layered Curriculum*.

I could see that the more reasonable solution for successfully including all types of learners was to modify the entire curriculum rather than make individual accommodation. These so called *whole-class* curriculum modifications make inclusion and teaching in the regular classroom so much more enjoyable. The method I designed and have used for several years in my own classroom is a method I now call *Layered Curriculum*.

Layered Curriculum is so named because the entire curriculum is presented to students in three layers. Each layer represents a different type of thinking or depth of study on a topic or unit of learning. Students work their way through a topic by gathering information on that topic, applying or manipulating that information and then critically thinking about an issue currently related to that topic. (Think Bloom's Taxonomy).

To build a Layered Curriculum, I simply took what I wanted my students to learn and do with that learning and broke it up into three main areas or layers based on where the learning fit in complexity. The bottom layer required students to add to their bank of knowledge, learn basic facts, rote information and basic skills. The middle layer asked students to play with their new knowledge, manipulate it, hook it to prior or concurrent study. The top layer asked students the big world questions - critical analysis and leadership decision making skills.

Originally the model was triangular shaped, with the bottom layer being the largest and most emphasized. We'll later see how often times the middle or top layer should be the largest. But as I designed this in my 10th grade biology class with state assessment tests which emphasized basic knowledge, that's where we begin.

As I'll discuss in detail later, Layered Curriculum uses a different paradigm for grading as well. I designed the model with an emphasis on student learning and accountability. Rather than the traditional grading system based on a percent of information recalled, the grading in Layered Curriculum reflects the student's depth of study and actual learning. The higher the grade, the deeper understanding a student has demonstrated.

As the design for Layered Curriculum began to form in my mind and in my classroom, a wealth of information and research coming from the field of neuropsychology helped shape the method as well.

We could have saved you but you cut us down, and soon you will be cut down and there'll be none of us to save you.
- John Steinbeck, Grapes of Wrath.

Chapter Three

The Biology of Layered Curriculum

The last two or three decades have brought an abundance of new research on brain function and learning styles. Neuropsychology and educators are still digging through all the results trying to make sense out of it all and understanding how best to apply it in the classroom. However, some of the main ideas that continue to come from the research are easily implemented in our classrooms. Some of this research supports what we already know and some is shedding new light on old problems.

The Issue of *Choice*

There are many parts to students' brains. But two most critical to the classroom are the cortex and the hypothalamus. The cortex is the top layer of the brain. It is the squiggly mass you see when you look at the brain and the part most of us think of when we think of a brain. It is actually a very thin layer of tissue, just six layers thick which wraps and covers the more primitive layers underneath.

The cortex houses most of our learning. This is where you store all your algebra, history, English, physics, knitting instruction, Barney songs, etc. Everything you "learn" is stored, for the most part, in the cortex. As classroom teachers, this is the part we are trying to reach. Unfortunately, due to the way the brain works, we have to get through the more primitive layers in order to reach the cortex. It would be handy for educators if the brain's priorities were top-down, but fortunately for our survival, the priority is bottom-up. Let me clarify.

As I mentioned, the parts underneath the cortex are more primitive. By that I mean we share those underneath parts with more primitive animals, they develop first and they "fire" or react first. These areas are basically responsible for our physical survival. They keep us alive in this world by running our bodies, regulating body activity, and reacting to life-threatening events in our environment. If there's time left-over, we can involve our cortex. So, in order to reach the cortex to store information on Civil War battles, we must make sure that the remainder of the brain is assured of basic survival.

One of the key players in survival, is a small area of the brain called the **hypothalamus**. Lying underneath the cortex, the hypothalamus controls a great deal of primitive needs. It is in charge of the primitive emotions - anger, aggression and fear. It also controls the fight or flight response, hunger, thirst, the sex drive, body temperature, water balance and the endocrine system of hormones. That's a lot of responsibility for a small region of the brain.

Apparently you are born with the hypothalamus up and running and ready for survival. It is the most primitive area of the brain that controls behavior. It generally reacts first in any situation perceived as threatening. Most of us are familiar with the sudden engagement of our hypothalamus (just think of the last time an event made you angry or very frightened). While the primitive survival brain areas are engaged, the rational thinking logic of the cortex is basically ignored as the "survival-at-all-costs" logic of the hypothalamus is in charge (again, just think of the last time an event made you very angry or very frightened). Often times the behaviors exhibited by an individual during "hypothalamus engagement" may not be judged as behaviors best suited in the long-run (are you thinking of the last time an event made you angry or frightened?).

Perhaps you see now, how teaching is difficult when surrounded by a group of students with their *hypothalamus engaged.* Some students (and adults) spend an awful lot of time using this part of their brain. They are called hypothalamus-driven individuals. I'm sure you know many of them (they seem to accumulate in 7th period). What causes this type of personality? A variety of factors enter into the display of primitive emotions, but one of the main reasons has to do with the basic biology of the brain.

The brain is nothing more than a mass of nerve cells, called neurons, held together with some glial cells. Whenever you think a thought, you are basically just firing a pathway of neurons through your brain with electricity and chemicals. The more often you fire a pathway, the easier it gets to fire. So the more often you look at someone's face, the easier it is to recognize. The more often you hear a tune, the easier it is to sing along, and so on.

This works in all parts of the brain. So those people who live in "fight or flight" worlds spend a lot of time firing pathways in the primitive regions of their brain. The more it's fired, the easier it is to fire and the more likely it is to fire. So if you have students whose home and family life revolves basically around eat-or-be-eaten, they are likely to be hypothalamus-driven individuals. Their brains easily fall into survival mode and their behaviors reflect that.

So, what's a teacher to do? It boils down to one simple word. Control. People want **control**. A feeling of control is a feeling that one's survival is not threatened. All of us want control, because that is what satisfies the hypothalamus and allows us to use other parts of our brain, mainly the cortex. Satisfying the survival needs of the brain should be the first priority of a classroom teacher. If the primitive regions aren't content, the cortex will not respond to teaching. The first thing which needs to be done is to establish an environment of trust, safety and the perception of control. If we are in control, our survival is not threatened, we are free to learn, create and grow.

The easiest way to allow students to feel control in the classroom is through choice. When students get to make choices in a classroom, they feel in control. When they feel in control, they take ownership in the activity and the behaviors exhibited are rational, logical behaviors determined by the cortex as opposed to the more primitive subcortex regions. When teachers allow students that type of control, the entire dynamic of the class changes. The *us-verus-them* mentality disappears, teachers are seen by students more as a coach on their side, learning is facilitated, and teaching is fun.

✧

And so this complex neuroscience information contributed to the development of Layered Curriculum and student choice became one of the cornerstones

The design is one of a completely student-centered classroom which holds students highly accountable for learning, makes students responsible, allows the teacher the role of facilitator, and encourages complex thinking. The following chapters will focus on each of the three layers, defining its purpose, design and grading.

Chapter Four

The Bottom Layer-- The C Layer

The bottom layer is called the *C layer* because the highest grade a student can receive by working solely in this layer is the grade of "C". All students will begin in this layer and work their way up. The purpose of this layer is to provide an opportunity for students to get a general understanding of the topic. This layer asks the student to collect factual information on a topic in a learning style, reading level, and language which is most comfortable to him or her.

Students work through this first layer by choosing from a variety of assignment choices offered in a written menu format called a **unit sheet**. Just like on any menu, you don't order everything. Students will pick and choose their way through the menu earning as many points as they like, up to but not surpassing a grade of C.

Different assignments are worth different points based on their complexity. Difficult, higher ability assignments are worth a lot of points, simpler assignments are worth fewer points.

Try to include 3 or 4 times as many assignment choices as you expect students to do. For example if you expect students to complete 4 assignments in this *C layer*, have them choose from a list of 12 -16 assignment choices.

Accommodating Different Learning Styles

As the *C layer* is constructed, try to list assignment choices that will favor a wide variety of learners. There should be something in this layer that meets the needs of every child you have in your room.

Therefore, *C layer* assignments will include choices for ***visual learners***. Assignments appropriate here would be textbook readings and questions, videos to watch, magazine and newspaper articles to summarize. Demonstrations, computer programs and art projects would also be appropriate for visual learners.

The *C layer* also includes assignments for ***auditory learners***. These assignments might include live or audio-taped lectures or readings, discussion groups as well as videos. Students with ADD/ADHD seem to enjoy taped lectures which they can listen to with headsets. The headsets help block out other distractions.

The bulk of the assignments in the *C layer* should be for ***tactile learners***. Remembering that in most general classrooms they make up the majority of learners, don't skimp on these assignments. Many of the assignments given for visual and auditory learners may include tactile learners as well. Appropriate assignments here would be art posters using various mediums, models, clay sculptures, drawings, computer work, flash cards, or vocabulary string boards, mobiles, bulletin boards and dioramas. Tactile assignments are particularly important if you have students who are poor readers or students with limited English proficiency.

In addition to addressing the needs of various learning styles, the *C layer* should include one or two assignments that can be done in a language other than English. These may include a written report or summary on a lecture, video, or even previous knowledge. The important thing here is to allow feelings of self-efficacy in your English as a Second Language (***ESL***) students.

An unexpected advantage I found to these ESL assignments was that most of my ESL students are first generation American. These students can speak their native tongue, but often cannot write in it, but someone at home usually can. I find students asking if they can take the assignment home, work with their parents and have some other family member write the assignment which they would then bring back and read. This was a wonderful opportunity to involve cross-cultural families in school and homework activities.

Right about now is when most teachers start to seriously wonder how we're going to grade all this! We'll get to that (the best part) in a minute.

One of the most important things you can do in a Layered Curriculum classroom is to use a wide *variety of textbooks* and reading sources rather than the traditional classroom set of books. In my general biology classroom I may have 25 different biology textbooks. I have some at a college reading level, many at various high school reading levels and some general science books written at an elementary level. This same idea holds for all the reading material. So although I get the newspaper, *Time* and *Scientific American*, I also get *Ranger Rick* and occasionally, *My Big Backyard*. This way I'm assured of having something at a reading level for everyone. This also provides "reading material" for non-readers.

I like my students to view the textbook as just one of many places to gather information, not our sole source. The easiest way I've found to do that is by not using class sets of textbooks.

Once again, each assignment is worth a certain number of points based on the difficulty of the assignment and how much time it requires. Students will not do all the assignments, but rather, choose several to accumulate the number of points they want. There are a minimum amount of points required as well as a maximum.

Remember, this layer is designed for general collection of information. Students are free to search for and gather a wide variety of information pertaining to the unit. You may want to involve the students in designing assignments, especially later in the year as students become familiar with Layered Curriculum.

Grading the *C Layer*

One of the keys and probably the founding cornerstone to Layered Curriculum is in the assessment. All assignments at this *C layer* are graded through an **oral defense**. At first glance, this may appear to be an overwhelming task, but is actually easily managed. This is the main facilitation role of the teacher and will take the bulk of your class time.

As independent work time begins, I start in one spot in the room and move sequentially around the classroom stopping to visit with each student to check progress or learning. As students complete an assignment I simply ask them a few questions about what they've learned. It takes about a minute to assess whether or not learning has actually taken place. For example, in my classroom, textbook questions are worth 15 points. To grade this assignment, I simply pull a chair up to the student's desk, pick up the questions, choose three at random, and we have a discussion. The student earns five points for each question he answers correctly. I may ask for clarification or a different explanation on any question to make sure the student understands what he is talking about. If two students worked together on the assignment I may do the assessment separately or together as a discussion with students adding to their classmate's response. The point here is to see what learning has taken place.

To give you another example, flash card vocabulary assignments are worth 10 points. I take the flash cards, choose 5 cards at random and ask the student the words. She will earn 2 points for each word she can define for me. So if she knows only 1 of the 5 cards I have selected she has a choice of taking the 2 points or taking her flashcards back and studying them a bit longer.

As we all know (or should know) the purpose of doing flashcards is not to *"do"* flashcards. It is rather to learn the vocabulary words. So the points come from the "learning" not from the "doing".

Be forewarned, in the beginning you'll get a lot of "you mean I did all those for nothing?" types of questions. The sad part of this is that students do not understand that if they did not learn anything from an assignment, then it really was all for nothing.

Students have just become accustomed to getting credit for "doing" an assignment. "Well I did it, doesn't that count" has become a frequent cry. In reality, sometimes "doing" an assignment just means that a students knows who to sit with at lunch before class time! And what we see too often is a student who "does" a lot of assignments and therefore accumulates a lot of points which offset low test scores and somehow comes out with a passing score at the end of the term. That right there is how we get students through grades and subjects learning very little. There is no accountability.

We hear the call for accountability a lot these days in education but unfortunately it isn't aimed at the right target. State, district, school, and teacher accountability are familiar terms, but student accountability is the piece that is missing.

One of the most failed parts of the education system is that we have put the emphasis for far too long on the process and have lost sight of the product. We only say to students, "Did you do your homework?" We rarely say to students "What did you learn from your homework?"

This critical part of Layered Curriculum is a complete shift in thinking on the part of student and teachers. The emphasis here is on learning and student accountability. Credit/points/marks are only earned through learning. *How* the student learns is not an important issue in the process, only that he or she learns. Your role is to help students understand the purpose of an assignment. And that purpose should be some type of learning or skill mastery.

Make sure you give students fair notice of this. At the first of the year, I explain the Layered Curriculum model to my students thoroughly. They know that they will get credit for learning something, not for simply doing an assignment. This still may be a point of serious adjustment on the part of the student for the first several weeks.

It is critical that you share your grading criteria with the students at the beginning as well. Grading rubrics or standards should be given to students in a written form with clear explanations. They should know going in what is expected and how they are to be graded. Grading and rubric examples will be discussed in a later chapter.

Logistics of Oral Defense

The bulk of my class time is spent in this type of one-on-one or small group dialogue. After a brief lecture and time for students to get their materials, I begin in one corner of the room and work my way around in a sequential manner, stopping to check on each student. I facilitate, direct, encourage, and grade completed assignments. As I am grading individuals, everyone else continues to work on their own assignments.

There are so many benefits to oral assessment that one has to actually try it to truly understand the difference. The first benefit is that it is generally a less stressful type of assessment than a formal exam. Since stress is one of the biggest suppressors of memory retrieval, most students benefit from this alternate testing strategy. An informal discussion with the teacher often allows them to convey what they have truly learned and any new thoughts generated on a topic.

Oral assessment also allows the teacher to quickly monitor whether students are understanding a topic or whether it is time to go back and review.

I remember the years when I gave written formal tests to my general biology classes. I would work so hard on designing the exam, but was always disappointed with how few students actually studied for it. Many would simply guess at the multiple choice and leave all the free response questions blank. Even the comments I wrote on the tests during correction were seldom read. I found that the time span between test and results was often too long to be meaningful. With face-to-face dialogue I don't encounter these problems. I can immediately correct errors, I can encourage deeper thought and explanation and I can help tie together the idea of class assignments and learning. Eventually students actually start asking themselves before they begin an assignment, "What I am supposed to be learning from this?" What an exciting difference.

The biggest benefit of oral assessment is the joy it brings to teaching. Many teachers haven't given much thought as to why they enjoy teaching, but I'll bet it's not because they love faculty meetings or filling out attendance records. The real joy of teaching comes from building relationships with wonderful young people and hoping that just one thing you say today will make a difference or ignite a spark in one mind. When you visit every day with every student you magnify the opportunity for this joy and fulfillment.

As I mentioned in the first chapter, relationship building is critical in the learning experience. So often, especially in large secondary schools, students come to school, go through six or seven periods, go home at the end of the day, and no one has even acknowledged their presence. For many children simply getting up, dressing and arriving on time is a big accomplishment, given the homes and family situations they are living in. How tragic that we can allow that effort to go unrecognized. So if only to say "welcome, thanks for coming, I'm so glad you're here", oral assessment is a good thing. As I move around my classroom, checking on the progress and work of students, I visit with everyone. It allows me to have some sort of exchange, no matter how small, with every student, every day.

I must caution here how important it is for the students to remain at their desks and the teacher moves through the room for oral assessment. I've seen some classrooms using Layered Curriculum where the teacher sits at his or her desk and the students come up there when they need assessment. There are many hazards to this process. It is difficult for the teacher to monitor the whole room, students get missed, time is wasted, facilitation is limited. Let the students stay where they are. You move. Make sure to check on everyone to make sure they are making progress and making good time management decisions.

If you get in a time crunch with oral defense (which is extremely common in the beginning) don't panic. You will find that oral defense gets easier and faster with each unit. In the beginning you may not want to try to talk to every student every day about every assignment. Work up to that goal. At first you may want to just quickly check daily progress and try to orally discuss one assignment each week with a student. Don't be afraid to try doing small group discussion, cooperative group assessment, quick written quizzes and other ways to check for learning. The point here is to increase accountability and get the students to understand that a relationship exists between school work and learning.

Lectures and Other Whole Class Instruction

Teachers frequently ask if I lecture to my students or do any type of whole class instruction. The answer is absolutely - I lecture everyday. However, the lecture is offered as an optional assignment in the *C layer*. It is always listed as assignment number 1 in the C layer: Listen to the lecture and take notes and it is worth 5 points per day.

At the beginning of each class period I announce the topic of the day's lecture and point out the outline for it on the overhead screen. Anyone choosing to do that assignment should move to where they can see the outline and anyone not doing that assignment is free to work on some other assignment quietly until we get finished.

I spend about 10 to 20 minutes lecturing. Students can listen and take notes, or quietly work on some other activity. The surprise here is that all the students choose to do that assignment! All of them. They quietly listen and take their notes from the outline. Compare this scenario to if I had mandated the note taking which is typically what happens in a teacher-centered classroom. If I had said, "I'm lecturing today and you need to take notes on this overhead outline. Please get out something to write on and no talking" I would now have a very different looking classroom. Suddenly about half of them would need a nap and the other half would remember that they needed to reorganize their purse or backpack.

The only difference here is the perception of choice. In one instance the students perceive they made the decision and in the other instance the students perceive I made the decision. Notice that the reality has not changed, only the perception. It's amazing what happens when you give students choice. As mentioned in the last chapter, giving choice puts students in control. They choose whether or not to listen. Because it's their choice, not mine, they take ownership and interest.

Of course, they also learn that I cover a great deal of information in those lectures which they will need in order to complete other assignments on the unit sheet. They also must be present to get credit for notes, so this helps reduce problems with being tardy. If they are absent or late, they are welcome to copy notes from a classmate so that they will have the information for their other assignments, but they do not get the credit of the lecture notes.

Completing the *C Layer*

Once students fulfill their *C layer* requirements they are ready to move on to the next layer. The number of assignments or level of mastery required is up to the individual teacher. Most teachers (myself included) allow partial credit for assignments. Some teachers require more of an all-or-none mastery to sign off an assignment. Use what works best for you and for your population. When students earn partial credit for an assignment in my classroom I explain what they would need to do to get the remaining credit and allow them to re-work/study or move on to something else.

All students will begin in this layer. Teachers frequently ask whether or not very bright students can simply skip or place out of this bottom layer. The purpose of this layer is to add to your knowledge base on the subject. All students can do that. Even your brightest student doesn't know everything on the topic so require them to add something. A heavily weighted quiz in this layer may help extremely knowledgeable students get through the layer quickly but I still think some new information should be gained before moving on.

As students discuss their assignments with you, initial and sign off the assignment right on their unit sheet. Log the points next to each assignment so that students have an obvious graphical reminder of where they are in the point scheme.

All students are expected to move to the next layer. One of the most common questions I get is from teachers wanting to know what to do with students who finish the *C layer* and then quit. First of all, do not allow that as an option. Classrooms are not student lounges. If students are in the classroom they are expected to be working. At no point would I allow a student to stop working with time left on the unit. As you'll see in the next chapter, you can help students move along through the layers by keeping the middle layer interesting and unusual.

C Layer assignment suggestions for visual learners

Here are some suggestions for types of activities and assignment choices that would be found in a *C layer*.

Traditional Textbook Use

- Read the chapter.
- Read and summarize.
- Read a section and discuss in a jigsaw group.
- Read and answer the questions at the end.
- Read and be prepared to answer the questions at the end.
- Read and be prepared to explain any illustration.
- Read the chapter and take a publisher made quiz.

Magazines articles

- Read the article and give me a 60 second summary.
- Read the article with a friend, each take an opposing point and debate it.
- Read and write a one paragraph summary of the main idea.
- Read the magazine and answer the worksheet.
- Find a magazine article on this topic. Highlight the key ideas.

Newspaper articles

- Read the article and give me a summary, written or oral.
- Find a newspaper article on this topic, highlight the important points. Prepare to discuss it with me.
- Find a newspaper article, clip it and give a 60 second summary to the class.

Video

- Watch the video.
- Watch the video and take notes.
- Watch the entire video and write 15 interesting things you learned from it.
- Watch the video and take a quiz at the end.
- Watch the video and fill out the worksheet.

Demonstration

- Watch and contribute to the discussion.
- Watch and then make one of your own.
- Watch the demonstration then use the ideas in one of the labs.
- Watch the demonstration and complete the worksheet.

Computer Program

- Work the program and summarize the key ideas.
- Work the program and fill out the worksheet.
- Work the program and take a quiz at the end.

C layer assignment suggestions for auditory learners

Taped textbook reading

- Listen to the textbook reading and follow along in the book. Do the end of the chapter questions on paper.
- Listen and follow along with the reading. Do the activities as indicated on the tape.
- Listen and follow along with the reading. Be prepared to orally answer the end of the chapter questions.

Lectures

- Listen to the lecture and take notes.
- Listen to the lecture and fill out the outline.
-

Debates

- In a group of four, plan a debate. Use at least 3 sources of information for your point and document it. Be prepared to debate on day 4.
- Read the magazine article with a friend. Each of you take a side and debate it. Be prepared to summarize the points of the debate.

Song Writing

- Write a song on (Arthropods). Include at least 10 new facts in the song. Perform it for me or 3 classmates.

C layer assignment suggestions for tactile learners

Computer programs

- Work the computer program and fill out the worksheet.
- Work the computer program and take the quiz at the end.
- Work the program for 30 minutes and be prepared to tell me 10 new ideas generated.

Flash cards

- Make flash cards using the vocabulary terms on the board. Learn them.
- Make flash cards using any 15 key terms from the chapter. Learn them.

Bulletin board construction

- With a partner, design and display a bulletin board showing (the process of photosynthesis).

Posters

- On poster board, make a full color poster showing (the taxonomic divisions in the plant Kingdom).

Dioramas

- Construct a diorama for any scene in the book.
- Working with 3 classmates, each construct a diorama depicting (a different major biome). Be prepared to discuss differences.

Constructing books/booklets

- Make a booklet persuading (a vote for water fluoridation).
- Design a booklet as (Samuel Adams may have for the colonists to incite a revolution).
- Design and illustrate a children's book on(how to prevent disease).

Collagés

- Make a collage using 3 different mediums showing (smoking propaganda).
- Work with a partner to make a collage (debating the draft). Each person take an opposing side.

Mobiles

- Make a mobile of (the Order Hymenoptera).

Models

- Build an edible model of (a cell).
- Build a model of (an amniotic egg) using material other than paper.

Board games

- Construct a board game teaching (cell division). The game must teach all stages. Have 2 classmates play the game.

Now is the time to make justice a reality for all of God's children. - Dr. Martin Luther King.

Chapter Five

The Middle Layer: The B Layer

The purpose of the middle layer is to have students apply, manipulate and play with the new information learned in the bottom layer. This **B layer** is designed to give students an opportunity to hook new information to existing knowledge or previous learning. Students can really make the learning personal and unique in this layer. The layer requires a more complex kind of thinking. I will remind you of this again, but it is important to note that the middle layer doesn't require *more* work, but rather *more complex* thinking. The layer is called the *B layer* because students wanting a grade of a "B" are going to have to work into this layer. This *B layer* asks students to **apply, manipulate, discover, hypothesize and prove, demonstrate, or problem solve**. Interdisciplinary assignments are wonderful in this middle layer. The layer may or may not be smaller than the C layer depending on where the emphasis is in your subject and curriculum, as we'll see later.

In the original design for my science class, I could easily see that the *B layer* was the place to put problem solving laboratory activities. But I wanted true problem solving, as opposed to traditional lab work out of a lab manual. A lab-manual type "cookbook" lab, while proclaiming problem solving, really is not. It generally provides a complete list of materials needed. It also includes a step-by-step procedure and a proper format for presenting data. After measuring, mixing and doing "something" according to the written instructions, students might answer some questions posed at the end which asked for reflection on what they've done.

This is not problem solving. These prepared labs require little original thinking on the part of the student. I want students to really think and problem solve here. So, for my *B layer*, I simply pose several questions. These are written in the middle layer on the unit sheet. The questions involve materials readily available in the classroom or community. The students choose one question to answer. It is important to only provide the question. I do not help with their procedure or solution. I will help them gather needed materials, but they must tell me what those materials are.

Here are some examples of *B layer* questions I've used in my general biology class:

> - How fast does a worm move in m.p.h.?
> - What percent of a plant is water?
> - How much weight can a snail pull?
> - Does water temperature affect plant growth?
> - Which holds more water proportionately, a paper towel or a natural sponge?
> - Who jumps further proportionately, you or a cricket?
> - Does Scope really kill bacteria?
> - Do Rolaids reduce acid levels?

In the beginning, students will naturally ask for help, with questions like "How do I do the one with the snail?"

My response is "I have no idea, that's your problem to solve."

You may imagine that at the start of the year, this creates a great deal of frustration on the part of the student.

Expect responses like "You're the teacher, you're supposed to help us," or "If you don't know, how are we supposed to figure it out?"

My response continues to be "I won't help you with ideas, but I'll be happy to help you with materials when you decide what you need." You know you are succeeding when you hear students proclaim "Well, don't ask her, she won't help." It may take several attempts before the students will give up on you for procedures and have to resort to using their own brains for problem solving. They may even begin to realize that school is for the students, not the teacher.

I might also make the point here that I frequently ask questions that I do not know the answer to myself. I simply sit around on the weekends and think up fun questions that a 16 year old might like to play around with. The great part about not knowing the answer myself comes at the end. When students finish a lab, they always want to know "Is that the *right* answer?" I can reply, "I don't know, I was asking you!" It always takes them by surprise. But, the student is finding out that real problem solving doesn't always have a *right* answer and that teachers may not always have the answers either. Sometimes we enjoy learning right along with the students.

Obviously labs may not be appropriate for all subjects and disciplines. The *B layer* in other subjects may ask students to demonstrate a skill, show mastery, exhibit a summation, perform, elaborate, compare and contrast. Basically in this layer you want students to play with their knowledge and hook it into a wide assortment of existing information they have. Design assignments where the products will be a unique creation from the student's unique perspective.

Grading the B Layer

Grading *B layer* problem-solving activities is relatively easy. You can assess them in a number of ways. You may again use an oral defense and have students discuss their work with you. This works well with younger students, students who struggle with writing, or any population where an oral defense would be preferable. You can have the students write their work up in a formal presentation or make a display and share it with a small group of classmates.

For a problem solving lab, I ask students to write five things:

1. What were they trying to find out? (question)
2. What did they think would happen? (hypothesis)
3. What did they do? (procedure)
4. What happened? (results)
5. Were they correct? (conclusion)

I also discuss their work with them, especially if they've worked in a group. Credit is given based on the logic they used in designing their procedure and their explanation. Their results must also be reasonable.

Reasonable is generally defined by me. For example, let's look at the problem of "how fast does a worm move in m.p.h.?" Suppose a group of students finish that lab and tell me that the worm moved 764 miles per hour. Well, I don't really know how fast a worm moves, but my guess is that it's not quite that fast! We might want to go back and re-examine their procedure. But if the answer looks reasonable and they've managed a logical attempt at solving the problem, they've passed this assignment.

Again, the objective of this layer is student engagement in and original application of knowledge gleaned in the *C layer*, or discovery on the part of the student. Assessment is looking for that. Has the student done some original thinking? Have they processed information and then applied it in a creative manner? This level should demonstrate learning beyond the rote storage of facts which was done at the *C layer*.

The *B layer* doesn't have to involve a lab. Depending on your subject, look for ways in which the students can creatively apply information they learned in the *C layer*. Have them design a geometric plan using new math concepts. Have them write stories using new vocabulary words. Have them apply concepts learned into a work setting. Each student product should be unique in that it is the product of their unique mind. For that reason it is difficult to grade based on the idea of right or wrong. Instead you are looking for a process.

This layer should also be enticing. The activities themselves should draw students up from the *C layer*. This helps prevent the beginning-of-the-year problem mentioned earlier of students finishing the *C layer* and quitting.

If you are having problems keeping the students moving along, re-examine your *B layer*. Try to think of something that a student would rather do than nothing. In working with adolescents I say, "think edible or gross". You want assignments out of the ordinary, something they can eat, something they must do outside, something requiring them to handle a disgusting cricket, etc. You want them to look forward to finishing the *C layer* so that they can get to the *B layer*.

B Layer Activity Suggestions

- Make a display for a class History Fair
- Demonstrate your skills
- Create a puppet show teaching the main points
- Conduct an experiment
- Build, Apply, Compare and Contrast
- Interdisciplinary projects
- Make a webpage or Power Point presentation
- Teach this through a 3-D bulletin board display
- ANY Interdisciplinary assignment works well in the B Layer

Mama exhorted her children at every opportunity to 'jump at de sun.' We might not land on the sun, but at least we would get off the ground. - Zora Neale Hurston.

Chapter Six

The Top Layer-- The A Layer

One of the ultimate goals of educators is to turn out students who can critically think about an issue in their lives long after their school days are over. Life calls upon us, sometimes daily, to make a **critical analysis** of an issue. The success of society depends upon its citizens to make critical decisions. We ask our leaders everyday to solve those problems for which there may be no clear right or wrong answer. Critical thinking requires the most complex kind of thought because it uses our entire brain - cortex and subcortex. The process implies that not everything can be found in the research. Sometimes we have to take the research and mix it with other things, like values, morality, ethics and personal opinion.

Critical thinking was the reasoning behind the start of public schools. Originally our job as educators was to make good citizens, good voters, good leaders and decision makers.

Even those of us who are not in a position to make national or even community decisions are faced with real critical thinking issues every day. Our old car breaks down and we have to decide whether to make an expensive repair or replace it. We are asked to vote on the person who can best represent us in government. A job opportunity arises and we must decide to take it or leave it. We give birth to a child with serious disabilities, how do we proceed in that child's best interest? These are the kinds of critical thinking tasks we must do in real everyday life.

One of the most common complaints among educators at all levels, from kindergarten to college, is that students can't or won't "think". What they are really complaining of is that students often lack critical thinking skills. Students must be taught the process of making a critical analysis. And that is what I ask my students to do in order to get an "A" in my class. Because the real world is full of *A layer* questions, it's never too soon to get started. The purpose of the *A layer* is to teach this process.

In the *A layer* we pose several questions which ask students to analyze a current or significant issue. Students then do research to get the current facts or expert information, and then use that research to form an opinion.

Questions at the *A layer* involve current event issues from the real world for which there may not be a clear right or wrong answer. These are issues of debate where you may find research to support more than one opinion or solution.

Some examples of questions I ask at this level are:

- Is stem-cell research a good idea?
- Pesticides - good or bad?
- When will we have a vaccine for AIDS?
- Should schools require the chicken pox vaccine?
- Was there ever life on Mars?
- What really happened to the dinosaurs?
- Is there a flesh-eating bacteria?

Again, the point here is to offer questions where students can find research for more than one side to the issue. The students working in this layer choose one question from a list of 2 or 3 questions - all of which do not necessarily have a right and wrong answer.

At the upper grades this assignment generally involves formal research. In the lower grades this may be done through alternate methods such as video documentary or student interviews. Students use an *A layer assignment sheet* (see end of this chapter) to help them document, summarize and cite their research. The assignment sheet asks for a summary of three recent magazine, reliable Internet, or journal articles on the subject.

In addition to summarizing each article, the students must also cite them correctly. This can be a challenge as many teachers know from the experience of seeing citations such as, "the computer in the library". Citing articles correctly is especially difficult given this day of the Internet. Many of us are not always sure ourselves of how to cite a particular reference. So, we spend time at the beginning of the year learning how to cite things correctly.

After researching, reading and summarizing three articles, the student must form an opinion on the issue. This opinion is written on the back of the form in two good paragraphs (defined as 3-5 complete sentences each). Students are graded on grammar, punctuation, supporting argument and spelling on this assignment.

All students can learn this procedure. All students, regardless of ability or disability can critically think. There may be a wide range in the sophistication of the thinking, but even students with serious mental disabilities can look at or listen to research summaries and then form their own personal opinion based on that research.

Grading *A Layer* Assignments

The *A layer* assignments in my classroom are always worth 20 points. You may find that you will have a very different point value for your *A layer* as we look at modifying units later in this book. On a 20 point assignment, students receive up to 5 points for each summarized article (2 points for a correct citation and 3 points for summary) and 5 points for their opinion. In order to get credit, they must form an opinion one way or the other on the issue. It doesn't matter what their opinion is or even whether or not it matches the research, but they do need to take a stand on the issue. While we can often see the validity in both sides of an issue we are frequently called upon to cast a vote.

A layer assignments can also be graded for issues such as sentence structure, grammar, spelling, punctuation, supporting argument and other points of value in your classroom.

While I find it nice to try to talk to students for a minute or so about their *A layer* assignment, these frequently are just graded in a traditional manner of having the student turn them in and I grade them on my own time. Time constraints may dictate whether or not I actually get to personally visit with students. Sometimes I do have them share their findings and thoughts with a classmate or in a small group discussion format.

Accommodating for Significant Writing Challenges

Occasionally I will have students in my class who have a writing disability. Writing is so slow or painfully difficult for them, that filling out the *A layer assignment sheet* would be an overwhelming task. In addition, I frequently have students who are extremely poor readers. For these students I make the additional accommodation that the *A layer* may be done orally. These students still must go through the same thinking / learning process of the *A layer*. So, even if a parent or resource teacher helps them find the information and even reads the articles to them, that student must be able to orally summarize the various pieces of research and argue the case for their opinion.

Separate grading rubrics may be designed for the oral presentation and you may find it best to offer both options to all students. As much as possible try not to stigmatize individual students with individual modification. If you need to offer an alternate form due to one student's situation it is usually best to offer it to everyone.

Sample   *A Layer* Assignment Sheet   20   points

Name_____

Unit #_____   Topic #____   Period:_____

Summarize 3 recent magazine or journal articles on your topic. On the back of this sheet write 2 good paragraphs (5 -7 sentences make a good paragraph) on your opinion. Make sure to mention some of the research in your opinion.

1.Title of Article:
Title of Magazine or Journal:
Author:
Date of Article:
Summary:

2.Title of Article:
Title of Magazine or Journal:
Author:
Date of Article:
Summary:

3.Title of Article:
Title of Magazine or Journal:
Author:
Date of Article
Summary:

Pay no attention to the man behind the curtain. - The wizard of Oz.

Chapter Seven

The Completed Unit

In it's traditional form, a complete Layered Curriculum unit is offered to students in a written format. The units are self-contained and include all possible options for how a student is graded. In other words everything that is done in class, from bell to bell should be put on the sheet with the point value. So if there are daily "class starter" quizzes, those should be included. If there is a formal exam at the end of the unit worth 50% of the grade, that too should be included. What you want is a clear picture for the student of the class expectations and a road map for their progress.

Because students will use their unit sheet to also log their progress, you need to leave room next to assignments for points to be recorded. Teachers have created all sorts of wonderful table and graphic designs for their units. Mine remain relatively plain and simple with the points possible listed after each assignment and a blank line in front of the assignment for my signature and points earned.

In the spirit of open information it's also important to include a due date and grading scale on the unit sheet. This allows students to constantly now where they are, where they are going, and when they need to get there. Here is a sample of a complete Layered Curriculum unit that I have used in my biology class. You will notice a due date, grade scale and points for daily lecture notes are written on the sheet. I also offer a place for parent signature so that parents can stay informed. This unit does not have a formal written exam at the end, but if there was one, it would also be noted at the bottom of the page. The whole point here is to eliminate surprise and mystery.

Fish & Amphibians: Conflict and Change

Student Name: _____   **Due Date:** February 24

Section I. "C" layer   65 points MAX in this layer.
1. Listen to the lecture & take notes (5 pts/day)   1   2   3   4   5
2. Write an autobiography. Include your name, age, your best physical feature, your favorite food, your favorite place to eat, describe your best friend and why, two conflicts you have in your life, where you go to feel the safest, and what you want to be doing five years from now. Write another autobiography. This time you are an amphibian. 15 pts.
3. Draw a water dwelling animal like a fish or octopus. Draw that same animal living on land. Describe the adjustments or adaptations that were made to move to land. This is an art project. It needs lots of art detail. Choose this only if you enjoying detailed drawing. 15 pts.
4. Quietly watch the movie, Toadspell. 5 pts.
5. After watching the video, Toadspell, write 2 paragraphs summarizing the movie and 2 paragraphs on conflicts you saw in the movie and how change resulted from those conflicts. 10 pts
6.. Listen to the recorded lecture on amphibians. Take notes. 15 pts
7. How is a frog like a fish (list 10 similarities). How is it different (list 10 diff). Must be done in a language other than English. 10 pts
8. Listen to the lecture on fish. Take notes. 15 pts.
9. Write a 10 sentence paragraph describing the difference between frogs and toads. Read it to 2 other classmates. Your paragraph must be in a language Other than English. 15 pts
10. Find 2 pieces of conflicting information on Fish or Amphibians between two textbooks. Explain why the books may differ on information. 15 pts
11. Watch any documentary-type t.v. show on fish or amphibians. List the title and date of broadcast. Describe the show in terms of conflicts in the amphibian world. 15 pts
12. Write a piece of poetry describing either conflict or change in an amphibian's world. Get written feedback from your English teacher. 15 pts
13. Read the chapter on Fish or Amphibians from the HBJ textbook. Outline the key concepts. Be prepared to summarize your reading. 15 pts.
14. Using adding machine paper, make a time-line showing when each vertebrate class appeared on earth. You must include a scale. 10 pts.

Section II. "B" layer   Choose One for 15 points
1. How fast does a fish swim in MPH?
2. Which moves faster, a fish or a frog?
3. How does water temperature affect fish?
4. With a classmate, Identify 15 key organs in a frog digestive system.

Section III "A" layer. choose ONE for 20 points
1. The science community is concerned over the apparent increase in physical deformities in North American frogs What are the causes?

2. Are EPA regulations sufficient in protecting fish from algae blooms?

3. What are some of the solutions to over fishing in our community?

Grading: 86-100 A   71-85 B   55-70 C   40 - 54 D

_____   _____

parent signature (5 pts in C layer)   Contact phone #

The above example illustrates the original *triangular shaped* model of Layered Curriculum the way it was designed in my high school biology classroom. The original intent was to accommodate both an increase in student learning and my state assessment test. Since the bulk of our curriculum and assessment covered basic content or *C layer* material, this had to make up the largest part of our learning time. So the model is triangular shaped because the largest layer is at the bottom. The C layer is where I put most of the points, most of my lecture and the bulk of our class time.

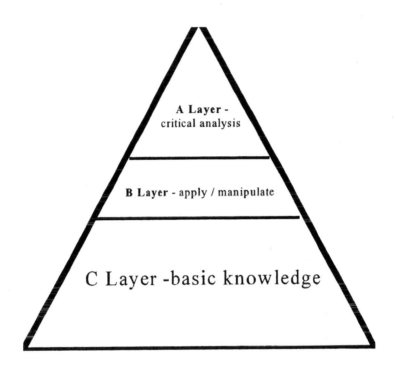

The model served me well for my high school general biology classroom. However, it wasn't long before other teachers took interest in the model and wanted to adapt it to a variety of subjects. So we began to look at different ways the design could be made to fit other subjects, other grade levels, other populations. It's these modifications which form the basis and emphasis of the 2nd edition of this text.

The two most obvious issues stood out immediately - not all subjects lend themselves to having the emphasis in the bottom layer and not all teachers were comfortable leaving everything optional. Others issues that have surfaced have been the mix of teacher directed and student directed assignments, interdisciplinary assignments and designing units for lower elementary grades. And thus the modifications began.

The 3 Keys to Layered Curriculum

The next few chapters will deal with modifications necessary for other subjects and grade levels. The best part of Layered Curriculum is that it does lend itself to individual teacher modification. But there are three things that must be present to be a true Layered Curriculum unit. They are the essential components or keys:

1. **Choice.** Student choice must be incorporated somewhere. Not necessarily everywhere but somewhere. Look for places where you can allow the students some choice in what they are doing. This is listed first and foremost as we know of nothing that changes the dynamic of a classroom more than this issue.

Student choice takes care of two big classroom problems: attention to the task and classroom management. People hear me say all the time "Creatures want control. If you don't give it to them, they look for ways to take it." Students are no different. The vast majority of classroom management issues are control issues. Give students the perception of some control and watch the whole room change instantly.

2. **Encourage higher level thinking.** Each layer should require more complex thinking on the part of the student. Layered Curriculum moves right along the lines of Bloom's taxonomy. Ask your students first to gather new information, then ask them to apply or manipulate that information and finally ask them to critically think about the topic.

Sometimes teachers will send me units of "Layered Curriculum" only to discover that what they've really designed are "Contract for Grade" units. Contract for Grade gives the students a long list of assignment choices and asked them to complete a certain amount for a grade of C, a few more for a B and a few more for an A. This is not Layered Curriculum. Layered Curriculum does not ask students to do additional work of the same level, but rather asks the student to think more complexly - elaborate, manipulate, grow more elaborate neural branches.

3. **Accountability.** Layered Curriculum units shift the emphasis of school work from "doing" to "learning". What we are really saying to the student is "here's what I need you to learn. I don't care how you learn it. I will offer you some suggestions on how others have learned this, but what's important is that you've learned it". Look for ways to give credit for actual learning, not just doing. Oral defense, small group discussion, quick daily quizzes can all be used to help students understand the true meaning behind school and home work.

Essential Keys to Layered Curriculum
- Choice
- Encourage more and more complex thinking
- Increase accountability

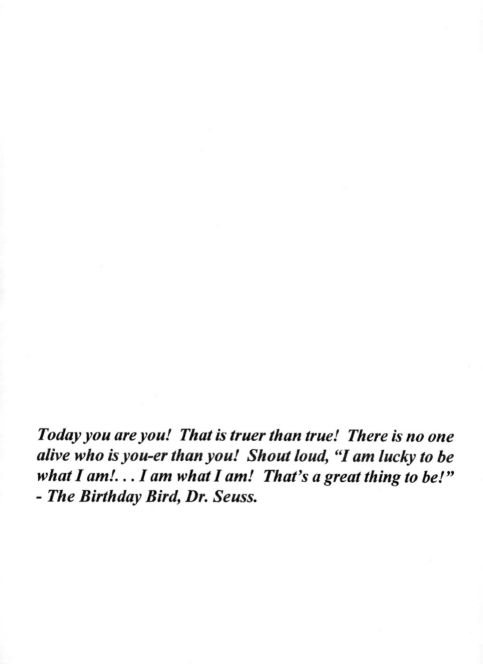

Today you are you! That is truer than true! There is no one alive who is you-er than you! Shout loud, "I am lucky to be what I am!. . . I am what I am! That's a great thing to be!" - The Birthday Bird, Dr. Seuss.

Chapter Eight

Changing the Shape - a Triangle Turns into a Diamond

Many subjects do not lend themselves to the original triangular shape of the Layered Curriculum model. The triangle puts the emphasis on the bottom, C layer, of learning. This works fine in basic classes where the curriculum dictates students learn a lot of basic information. If the state assessment, national exam or other evaluation for your subject asks students to simply memorize and regurgitate facts and basic knowledge, then the C layer covers that well with the triangular model.

But what if your emphasis lies in another layer?. The first place we encountered this was when we were adapting the model for technical classes, physical education and composition. If you are teaching a unit on poetry writing you definitely want students to read other types of poems and learn the basic styles of poetry, but your primary focus is on the students themselves actually applying the information by writing a poem of their own. In other words, the emphasis should be on the B layer, the application layer. And so the "diamond shaped" Layered Curriculum was born.

A diamond shaped model also has 3 layers each incorporating the learning and thought process found in the triangle - gather new information, apply that information, critically think. But the bulk of the class time, the bulk of the points, the bulk of teacher emphasis is on the middle layer.

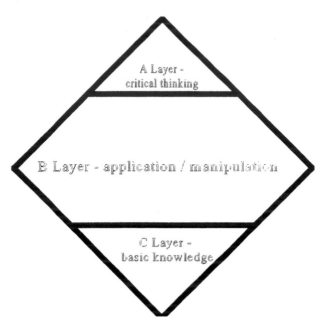

Many subjects lend themselves to this shape of model. English composition, technology, family and consumer science, physical education, industrial arts, the fine arts, all put a high priority on student application of new skills. For example it is easy to see that in a woodworking course you need to spend a fair amount of time on skills, safety and materials, but that what you really want the student to do is apply all that learning by building something out of wood.

Notice though that even with this shape, the evaluation or critical thinking process is still there. After all, an important part of learning woodworking is evaluating good projects from bad. Artists not only need to apply skills to their art, they need to be able to judge critically the use of those skills and expression in good art. So again, the three layers are still there, just in differing amounts.

Another factor that may influence the size of each layer is the grade level and age you are teaching. There's a good amount of writing in brain development that would favor teaching more of the basic knowledge component to children in elementary school, but allowing more opportunity to apply, manipulate and critically think about things at the secondary level. Abstract reasoning develops around age 11, so while younger children should get opportunities to practice adult thinking, the brain isn't mature enough to do it very well. So basic knowledge should be emphasized in elementary and most teachers find the C layer to be their largest layer in these grades. (See the chapter on adapting for Elementary)

Here's is an example of Layered Curriculum emphasizing the middle layer.

Constructing a Paragraph

Name_____ Date _____ Period _____

C Layer (minimum 15 - maximum 25 points)
1. Build vocabulary cards. (5 points)
2. Choose up to 2 worksheets: Find the topic sentence in each group of sentences. Arrange them so they form a paragraph. This is a "shared" assignment (5 points - each)
3. Choose an article from the box. Write a paragraph summary. . (10 points)
4. Working in a group, make a collage of well written paragraphs from magazines and/or newspapers. (10 points)
5. Participate in the class discussion on paragraph construction (2 days @ 5 points/day)

B layer - 50 points
1. Think of your favorite TV show. Summarize a recent episode in paragraph form. Use 7 - 10 paragraphs. (20 points)
2. Bring in examples of 10 paragraphs you have written in other classes. (10 points)
3. Group discussion - Use one of the "misprinted" stories from the box. Your team needs to re-write the story inserting paragraphs appropriately. (20 points)
4. Find any magazine article containing at least 20 paragraphs. Be prepared to discuss the reason for separating the ideas as they did. (10 points)
5. Write a story. Two typed pages. Must have a beginning, middle and end. Use paragraphs appropriately. (20 points)

A layer - 25 points
Find 3 good and 3 bad examples of paragraph use in the newspaper. Prepare your defense.

Chapter Nine

The right mix of required and optional assignments

A great many teachers, because of their grade level, subject matter, or teaching style cannot offer Layered Curriculum in a completely open and optional manner. Often times, certain material must be presented in a sequential manner or is best presented in a whole class method. In addition, many teachers are faced with liability issues, illiteracy, and school policy. Fortunately, the creative minds of teachers can work through nearly any obstacle.

Reminder: Not every assignment needs to be offered as an option. Some things can and should be required events or done all together as teacher led direct instruction.

Modifying for English Novels

If you are teaching the novel *Huck Finn*, it is difficult to leave reading the book as an optional assignment. So most teachers who successfully use Layered Curriculum have obviously made some parts of the unit required. Generally the first couple of assignments are required of all students - particularly the reading of the book! So, if you are teaching a unit on *Huck Finn*, the first assignments in your *C layer* may be required, as such:

#1. Read the book. (Required)
#2. Participate in class discussion.(Required)
#3. Do one character analysis. (Required)
4. Watch the video clip from one chapter.
#5. . . . . .

The rest of the unit sheet will be a variety of ways students can learn and think about the novel and they are free to choose from the remainder of the assignments to finish off their grade.

I know of some English teachers who have managed to work through the *reading* part of novel assignments by offering a choice in reading. They recognize that some students struggle with reading and the novel would take much longer to get through, and that many students prefer silent individual reading. In their classes, they offer the option of both.

To offer this option, the teacher reads the novel, once, onto a tape which is put into a listening center. Students may then sit at a listening center, using headphones and follow along in their novels, or they may use the time for silent individual reading. Either way, the novel is read and time is easier to plan. This is especially effective if you have a wide range of reading levels and abilities in your class.

Another creative option I have seen is the literature teacher "buddy teacher" system. Two teachers offering language arts or English at the same time period and reading the same book will team up and design a unit of Layered Curriculum together. During the reading time, one teacher will offer the "silent reading" classroom while the other teacher offers the "read aloud" classroom. Students move between the teachers during that time period. Teachers alter each day who has the read aloud and who has the silent reading classroom.

Modifying for Honors and Advanced Placement Classes

Honors and Advanced Placement (AP) classes are usually modified in the same way that we will modify for lower elementary and math - leave the *C layer* looking rather traditional.

I taught AP Biology for many years. The AP Biology curriculum is long, difficult, and perhaps most importantly, taught to a very specific national exam at the end. There is a tremendous amount of material which we have to get through. Even more of a factor, AP classes are frequently a very homogeneous a group of learners and therefore do not require so many assignment choices. So in modifying Layered Curriculum for these classes, the entire *C layer* is required of my students and presented as traditional *whole-class* instruction.

When I say *whole-class instruction* I mean that I do not present the *C layer* as options on the unit sheet. The assignments that I would normally put in the *C layer* are simply the basic class requirements with very little, if any, choice. Students are required to attend class, take lecture notes, read the chapters, and do a certain number of textbook review questions. Meeting these minimum requirements, however, will only get the student a grade of "C".

Anyone who knows students taking advanced classes knows that a "C" grade is simply not an option in their world. So the *B* and *A layer* is presented as a small section which gives them a choice of research, lab, and critical thinking questions which they can then choose from to finish off their grade. The *B and A layer* are similar to what I present to my general classes in terms of the thought processes involved. The B layer consists of problem solving lab activities which they do on their own or in pairs. The *A layer* assignments require library research and a critical analysis.

I also use oral assessment in grading the class activities for my AP classes. It is important to help students connect class and homework activities and learning.

In addition to class activities, labs and research, we have a formal written exam at the end of each unit which counts for half their unit grade. So a 100 point unit will come with a 100 point exam. The exams are traditional exams designed to mimic the types of questions found on AP tests. I include free response questions which the students read and grade themselves from a written criteria. Again, this is designed to mimic the AP testing situation.

Modifying for Liability Issues

What do you do if your subject includes things like power saws, Bunsen burners, open flame, chemical hazards and the like? Obviously the thought of letting students work independently while you are doing oral assessment across the room, probably terrifies you. It would me. Teachers with these issues have solved the problem by offering these assignment choices on certain days.

For example, in teaching a chemistry class, the labs would be done on a designated lab day.

The teacher can simply state "All labs will be done on Thursday of this week. If you are planning to do a lab on this unit, plan to do it on Thursday. I will not be correcting any other assignments on that day as I will be spending my time supervising the lab area."

You may need to offer lab days, cooking days, construction days, etc. more or less often depending on your subject. You may want to have entire class periods for lecture and some days with no direct instruction whatsoever. These days would be for student work or labs.

Obviously the number of lab days would vary from subject to subject. In hands-on intensive courses, you may need 4 out of every 5 days to be student lab days. There may be quite a bit of choice in the labs or projects students are working on, but you would simply supervise those activities as you would in any traditional type of classroom.

Chapter Ten

Modifying Layered Curriculum
for Other Issues

In addition to modifying for required versus optional assignments, you may find that you need to also modify the amount of variety needed in each layer, the length of the units, the amount of whole class instruction, and other issues that reflect your unique population and teaching situation.

Modifying for Traditional Versus Block Schedule

First we need to define block scheduling One of the things I've learned from traveling throughout the country and visiting schools is that every district has a different definition for **block scheduling.** I can remember more than one instance where I would start talking to teachers about teaching on a block and halfway through the conversation would realize that we were talking about completely different things.

Layered Curriculum was developed in a school that runs on an odd/even block schedule. This means that we met our students every other day for an 80 minute period. Students attend their odd (1, 3, 5, 7) period classes one day and their even (2, 4, 6, 8) period classes the next.

There are many versions of this expanded class schedule across the country. Some schools meet everyday for 80 minutes but the class lasts only half the year. Some schools meet odd-even blocks on Monday through Thursday with all classes meeting on Friday for a short 40 minute period. Some schools mix block classes meeting every other day with some shorter classes which meet every day. The variation is enormous.

Of course there is even variation in the **traditional school schedule**. Some schools run on 6 periods, some 7 and some even try for 8. I've seen schools that rotate the classes so each day starts with a different period. (This is an idea whose theory I love, but never having taught it, I think I'd go crazy). Then, there's all those divided lunch period options, but let's not even go into that. So your class periods are most likely in the range of 40 to 80 minutes, depending on the school.

I have had the opportunity to teach on only two of these types of schedules, the odd-even block which I'm currently on and the traditional six period day. I've used Layered Curriculum on both schedules and it works fine, although modifications are needed for the traditional school schedule.

On the block, I have time to lecture briefly every day, allow five minutes for planning and getting materials, and get around to every student at least twice before the five minute clean-up. It is the schedule I prefer. The 80 minute time span allows a great range of options for direct instruction and plenty of time for labs and other small group projects.

However, I was also able to work Layered Curriculum on the traditional 6 period day schedule. In that type of set-up, I would only lecture every other day. That left the "non-lecture days" with plenty of time for individual seat work and assessment. While we could get started on individual assignments on lecture days, the shorter period did not really leave sufficient time for much independent work. I could usually get around very briefly though to every student to at least facilitate and answer individual questions but saved most of my assessment work for the non-lecture days. Also, students were only allowed library time on the days where there was no lecture. I found that students who went to the library after the lecture did not have enough time in the library to make it worth their leaving the room. Certain days were designated as lab days.

Depending on how often and how long you meet your students, you may have to modify Layered Curriculum. But I've never seen a schedule that it can't work with. If you have long and short days mixed, you may try saving the short days for testing, lecture, and quizzes and keep the longer periods for student work, labs and research.

Modifying for Early Elementary

Layered Curriculum works beautifully in lower elementary classrooms. Again though, modifications are necessary. If you are using Layered Curriculum for a kindergarten or first grade class, the unit sheets are not written for the students, they are written for the teacher. The unit still requires (and reminds the teacher) the student to think through all three layers - gathering information & new knowledge, applying knowledge, critically thinking.

While most brain research supports a heavy time commitment for basic knowledge and rote learning in the lower grades, feel free to emphasize the middle or top layer on some units.

Elementary teachers also have the advantage of easily implemented interdisciplinary units. You may want to start with one subject units until you get the feel for the model and both you and your students are comfortable with the routine. Social studies is usually a good starting place. Then try putting a unit together mixing social studies and language arts. Obviously science and math make a good combination as well.

If you have a colleague at your school who is interested in teaming with you, try designing a unit together for one subject (say language arts) and implement the units at the same time of day. Divide up some of the activities between you and assign certain activities to certain rooms. Have the children mix between the rooms based on what activity they are choosing or put the children in mixed groups for assigned activities.

For example, I know of two 3rd grade teachers who run their language arts units together. Every day from 10:00 am - 10:50 is language arts. One room is designated as the "absolute quiet" room and the other is designated for assignments that require some student interaction. Students will mix between the rooms depending on what assignment they are working on that day. The plan gives children some exposure to other teachers and other classmates.

Elementary classrooms are generally set up with centers and students choose between 2 or 3 centers to achieve an objective. Centers may be color coded or labeled by objective. For example you may need the students to complete one blue center and one green center before morning recess. The blue centers teach fine motor skills and the green centers all teach journaling or writing skills.

Teachers have found all types of creative solutions for using Layered Curriculum and *keeping score* with younger children. The *learning centers* design is the most familiar solution for creating a classroom for non-readers.

You may want to use colored tokens, popsicle sticks, cards, etc. to help students keep track of objectives mastered and areas visited. All assignments designed to teach a specific objective would offer the same color token. Students need to collect tokens of various colors and the teacher can set policy as to how many and which color.

It is not important the manner in which you lead your students through the layers, only that they do get through all of them. Some teachers prefer to have students work through *C layer* activities all together using traditional direct instruction and then offer options only for the application and critical thinking. They may spend the first day on direct instructions followed by a couple of days of independent work on the application or small group work on the critical thinking. Some teachers offer C layer activities through centers and then do whole class critical thinking projects later in the week. The variety is endless and is up to the teacher's creative discretion.

The following is a sample of an early elementary unit. The unit is written for the benefit of the teacher and is really just a plan in how to lead students through the three basic layers of thinking.

The World of Cinderella Stories * (1ˢᵗ grade)

Note for teachers: Read different versions of the traditional story from different time periods. Some stories could include: Politically Correct Cinderella, Paper Bag Princess, CinderElmo, Irish Cinder Lad, Ruff Face Girl (Algonquin), Yeh Shin (Chinese) along with others noted, below.

*Required activity

C Layer : Traditional Cinderella Story & Other Cinderella Stories

*1. Listen to story read by the teacher
*2. Listen to The Korean Cinderella Story about Pear Blossom.
*3. Watch the video: "Mufaro's Beautiful Daughters"
4. Draw a picture of something that happened in one of the stories.
5. Look at a picture from one of the stories. Using the picture for help, tell the teacher something that happened in the story.
6. Write five to ten new vocabulary words from one of the stories.
7. Create a sequence of events of the story, from pictures you have drawn.

B Layer: Project

1. Fill in chart Comparing and Contrasting characters, events, setting, etc.
2. Create your own "Cinderella" story.
3. Make puppets, write dialogue, and do a puppet show for the class.
4. Make a craft from each version.

A Layer: Writing

1. Why do you think that people around the world have this similar story? And are they different?
2. How you would feel if you were Cinderella?
3. Do you think these kinds of stories really happen in real life?

* Contributed by Paula King, Massachusetts

Modifying for Home Schooling

Home-schooling teachers have many advantages, not the least of which is small class size! You also have the advantage of knowing the individual needs, talents, strengths and weaknesses of your students much more so than most teachers.

However, just because you know the likes and dislikes of your student, doesn't mean there is no place for choice. For the reasons mentioned so far in this book, choice should still be offered. Obviously you will not need a wide variety of assignments, but gently push your child to move out of his or her comfort learning style. Get them started and engaged in a learning style that they prefer, but ask them to move out of their comfort zone as well.

Much like we saw with early elementary, the thought process in designing Layered Curriculum for home schooling is more for the benefit of the teacher. What you want to make sure of is that the child has moved through all three layers. Give them an opportunity to gather new information on the topic, apply or manipulate that information and then critically think.

Give careful thought to what layer you want to emphasize. If your child is trying to catch up for a delay in an area, your emphasis may be in the bottom layer. If you are working with your child in a subject where she shows particular giftedness, you may want to emphasize the application, manipulation or critical thinking layers so that she can really diverge and elaborate on her knowledge base.

You may also want to heavily involve your child in the planning of the B and A layers. Perhaps as you both move through the *C layer*, ideas for projects and areas of elaboration will present themselves.

If you are home schooling a sibling group, find creative ways for student interaction on each layer. So even if you have one 1st grader and one 4th grader, design the social studies units or science units together, but with a variety of grade appropriate activities.

Remember too that field trips are a great way to gather information for the *A layer* assignments. Have your child interview people at various locations - gather information in the form of a field report to use in their analysis.

Modifying for Math

Many math teachers find that the easiest way to use Layered Curriculum in math is to leave the *C layer* looking fairly traditional. In other words, the *C layer* would have lots of daily direct instruction with assigned practice problems. So, the teacher would demonstrate a new skill each day or every other day and then assign students practice problems to work in order to learn the skill. You may or may not offer some choice in the practice activities. Thus far, it looks like a traditional math class.

However, student choice can certainly be added when it comes to introducing the next two layers. The *B layer* and *A layer* require manipulation/application and critical thinking and students are given some choices on topics and direction.

Some teachers offer a choice or two in the *C layer* practice problems, some don't. Some teachers offer a choice in homework assignments, some don't.

One of the most creative methods I've seen for assigning homework was to tell students to work the entire page of practice problems or as many as they needed to in order to master the skill (with some type of minimum number required). The following day students had a choice of how to earn their homework credit. They could either turn in the entire page of practice problems worked, or "pull a card" from a stack of 3 X 5 cards that had samples on them and work them to perfection. Either way earned the homework points. This really got the message across to students that the purpose of the homework was to build a skill.

Modifying for other sequential issues

You may wonder as you put your unit together how to make sure that students "get" certain information or skills or at least get a variety. . What if there are some skills they have to learn before they can learn another skill? What if there is a definite sequence to the learning within a unit? What if there are several objectives of the *C layer* that must be met? These problems are best addressed by sub-dividing the *C layer*.

Even if there are certain required concepts, you may be able to offer variety within the concept. For example, you may need everyone to learn vocabulary words, but there are several ways in which the students can learn them. Or they may need to learn lab safety, but can choose a variety of ways to do that. So your *C layer* may look like this:

C Layer
Choose ONE assignment from within each TOPIC.

Topic 1: Vocabulary
1. Make flashcards using your own definitions. Learn them.
2. Build a string board using the vocabulary terms.
3. Play the vocabulary quiz game with 2 other classmates.

Topic 2: Book work - Chapter 12
1. Make illustrations for 10 sections of the chapter summarize the main points.
2. Outline the chapter, paraphrasing the main ideas in each section.
3. Answer the end of the chapter questions.

Topic 3: Lab Safety
1. Watch the video on lab safety and answer the lab sheet.
2. Participate in the small group demonstration on Tuesday.
3. Read Appendix A in the text and fill out the worksheet

The list could go on for as long as necessary until you've covered all the main objectives you need covered. The *B and A layers* would tie together many of the objectives covered in the *C layer*. Once again, remember that sometimes you may just have to require some assignments.

Modifying for College and Adult Learners

Layered Curriculum is particulary useful in teaching adult learners. Adults, like children, are most creative when empowered with a sense of control. I have used a modified version of Layered Curriculum in several college classes that I have taught. It especially helps with the problems encountered in one night a week or all-day Saturday type classes.

Adults are a special student population in that they have other significant community responsibilities outside of the classroom (worker, boss, mother, father, spouse). Instructors must be especially mindful of the variety of ways in which these adults have included school into their lives. Some adults have extra time between classes to devote to the course, and some have very limited time outside the scheduled class time.

It has been my experience that due to their outside obligations, many adult learners are also fatigued during long class periods and may not work best during a long three to five hour session.

Therefore, you can start to see the possibilities that Layered Curriculum allows for in adult classrooms. Lectures may be optional and worth a certain number of points. Obviously most learners will attend the lectures as the material presented is important, interesting and beneficial. However, occasionally the student may have to miss class or come late due to some other unforseen obligation. This allows the student the option to make up those points with alternative assignments.

The same holds true with non-lecture activities such as group discussions, videos, and other activities held inside the classroom. The students can choose to stay and participate in the activities or if they have to leave early, or are simply too tired to fully participate one evening, other options are available for them with between-class activities.

Outside research projects are more productive when students feel they have a choice in the topic. Here you may want to offer three or four topic choices for the student. Instructors may also offer optional forms for research presentations - written report, display, or oral presentation.

In the college courses I've taught, I wrote up a unit of assignment options for each unit. It consisted of attending the lecture, films, outside investigations, journal research, projects from the textbook, groups discussions, video, etc. In the three hour course, my lecture and class discussion took the bulk of the time. However, the last part of the class involved one of the other activities. Students could stay and participate in the video, discussion, project, etc. or leave and do one of the outside projects during the week.

This worked very well in my class population. Students enjoyed having that choice and felt that the class really accommodated the needs of the adult learner. Some students had only that particular block of time allocated from work, children, and other responsibilities and stayed the whole class time to participate. However some, too tired that late in the evening, attended the lecture and discussion, but left early for home knowing they would have an activity to complete on their own during the week.

Chapter Eleven

Designing and Implementing your own Layered Curriculum Units

The first unit you design on your own will take you a long period of time. By "long period" I mean three or four hours on a Sunday afternoon. In all fairness, I must also warn you that your first unit may not be a total success. Most teachers tell me that their first unit was a bit messy, their second was almost workable, and by the third attempt they felt they got it.

The tricky part seems to be in getting the time and point system worked out. It is hard to judge how many assignments and how long to give students to work on the unit.

How to Begin Layered Curriculum Mid-year

If you are starting this in the middle of the school year, I strongly caution you against working up a full Layered Curriculum unit over the week-end, walking into your classroom Monday morning and handing it to your students with the instructions, "you've got 2 weeks, choose what you want, have fun." I believe your students would be slightly overwhelmed, to say the least. Don't do that.

Even when starting this at the beginning of the year, one has to move slowly and keep lots of structure and tight intermediate (or daily) deadlines. Students who are unaccustomed to working in student-centered classrooms need to be instructed in how to set their own pace, find materials and plan wisely. Unfortunately, students are used to having everything mandated and spelled out for them and accepting the responsibility for their own learning may take some time.

So my best advice for you is to start with what you do right now, and then add one piece. If you will slowly work into this student-centered model, you are more likely to find success.

Occasionally I will find teachers who can plunge right into this with many things going on in their room and do just fine. But I find these are teachers who had a bit of a busy, student-centered environment to begin with. Most teachers, on the other hand, use the familiar teacher-centered approach where they offer whole class instruction and then give a seat work or homework assignment for follow-up. So let's assume a start from this more traditional classroom.

An easy way to begin your Layered Curriculum evolution is to simply add a choice in the traditional seat work assignment. Start your class period with some teacher directed instruction - a lecture, demonstration, story, chalk-talk, etc. Then offer two assignment choices for the follow-up seat work.

You may find it easiest to divide your students into groups. "Those of you doing assignment A, please sit on this side of the room and those of you doing assignment B, sit on the other side of the room." Make the assignment due at the end of the period (or if it is lengthy, require a certain amount to be completed by the end of the period with the rest for homework). Structure and firm deadlines are critical when moving students from traditional teacher centered environments to more student-centered approaches.

After a few days of this strategy you can begin to add more and more variety as needed and eventually add your middle and top layers. Again, you may find it easiest to walk the students through those middle and top layers as a group in whole class instruction.

Beginning At the Start of the Year

If you are starting Layered Curriculum right from the beginning of the school year you can probably begin with a bit more variety and choice and you certainly can begin with all three layers on your first unit. I suggest, however, that you begin with the *daily method.*

The daily method of Layered Curriculum offers students limited daily choices. Teacher directed whole class instruction always begins the class period. Similar to the description above, the teacher would introduce a concept with a lecture or demonstration and then have the students look on their unit sheets for their Day One Activity Choices. Have them choose one of those assignments and require that it is due at the end of the period. After a few days of this *C layer* thinking, you move as a class, into the next layer. Work the *B layer* together as a class or in small groups on the same day and work the *A layer* together as a class. Whole-class *A layer* assignments can be done at the media center or the teacher can bring in the research to be used. Short video documentaries showing the research and views from different sides of an issue is an easy way to collect research for whole-class *A layer* assignments especially with young students or students with poor or limited reading and research skills.

With the daily method, what you are basically going to do is walk the students through a unit using a modified whole-class instruction approach. I've included an example of a unit I have used to introduce Layered Curriculum to my class at the end of this chapter. As you can see in the example, the unit is written over my usual five day time period.

The first three days we work on *C layer* assignments. I've taken the *C layer* for that unit and broken it down into manageable chunks. Students must choose one assignment each day to complete, in addition to lecture notes. Students may be overwhelmed with 20 choices, but most can easily choose from three or four choices. They can also understand having to complete one assignment during the class time and most are familiar with listening to a short lecture.

On the fourth day, the entire class works on a *B layer* assignment together. I walk students through the thinking process, assembling equipment, writing the lab and working it. We also go over how these assignments are graded and how to write them up.

On the fifth day, we all go to the media center to work on an *A layer* assignment together. Not only do they learn how to find resources, we discuss citation issues and review how to write a *good* paragraph and summary.

By the end of this first unit, all students are familiar with how the units work and are ready to do one on their own. Now, I can hand them a complete unit and they are not as overwhelmed. Occasionally, depending on the type of class, I will provide a second unit with the *C layer* assignments broken into chunks again. Some teachers use this daily method for the majority of the year.

If your students need a lot of structure, this is a great way to get it. If at any point you feel the classroom is getting out of control, or students have too much time, as seen by too much off-task behavior, etc., then revert back to this daily method for a unit or two. You want to help your students learn self-discipline and planning, but you also have to remember they are children and these skills are not smooth and mature. When they slip and fall, catch them and help them back up.

Here are a couple of sample units done using a daily method of Layered Curriculum:

The Arthropods -(grade 10 Biology)

All 5 days: listen to the lecture and take notes. 5pts/day
1 2 3 4 5

Day 1:
1. Quietly, watch the movie. 10 pts
2. Write 15 new ideas learned in the movie. 5 pts
3. Write a 2 paragraph summary of topics covered in the video. 5 pts.

Day 2:
1. Read the chapter in any textbook on Arthropods. Be prepared to answer the end-of-the chapter questions. 15 pts.
2. On butcher paper, illustrate a poster showing the classes of arthropod and 3 examples of each. 10 pts.
3. Listen to the audio-tape and answer the questions. 10 pts.
4. Make a 4 sided paper cube. List one Class of Arthropods on each side and draw a representative of each. 5 pts.

Day 3:
1. Make a mobile for the room showing the Orders of any Class of Arthropods. 10 pts.
2. Work the computer program. 10 pts.
3. Make flash cards of the vocabulary board terms. Learn them. 10 pts.
4. Do the worksheet packet for this unit. 10 pts.

Day 4: "B" level Labs 15 pts (choose one)
1. Who jumps further, proportionately, a cricket or a human?
2. What is the average speed of an ant?

Day 5: Choose One. Use an "A" level assignment sheet.
1. Is the risk of poisonous spiders in Utah greater than other states?
2. Does the shellfish industry seriously harm natural populations of the animals?
3. Can AIDS be transmitted to humans from mosquitoes?

86+ = A   71+ = B   56+ = C   40+ = D

Shelter - Science, grade 4*

Day 1
Listen to the story: A House is a House for Me
Read pages 5 -9 in the text, then choose one of the following:

1. Describe the homes of 3 animals you've read about or know of.
2. Illustrate 3 animals and their homes.

Day 2
Choose 1 activity from the list below. You may do the activity by yourself, with a partner, or in a small group of 4.
1. Watch the video clip about animal homes. Write a paragraph about what you saw.
2. Go to the computer and find the web site: thewayitworks.com. Investigate how an animal of your choice makes its home. Be ready to share the information with your class.
3. Meet with the teacher at the science table and investigate the bee's nest. Bring a piece of paper to write notes and draw sketches.

Day 3
Today everyone must do the same project. However, you may do it in any way listed below or in your own way if you have a better idea. Describe your house. Make sure you describe the rooms and what is inside your house.
1. You can write about your house. Make sure you use complete sentences.
2. You can draw your house. Make sure you accurately draw each room and what is inside of each room.
3. You can make a 3D model of your house. Make sure you include all rooms.

Day 4

Each person will share his or her house with the class. You must be able to answer all questions in front of the class. When everyone has had an opportunity to share you may choose one activity listed below.

1. Meet with another person from the class. Compare your house with theirs. Make a list of the things that are similar and the differences in each house. Come up with a list of 5 questions that you ask to find out more information about the other person's house.
2. Make a T-chart comparing your house with an animal's house. Draw the different parts directly across from each other so it is easy to see what you are comparing. For example: the entrance to the house, the place where food is kept, etc. Come up with 5 reasons why each house is suitable for its owner.

Day 5

Choose one question and answer it using the information that you learned this week and what you already know. You must write at least 2 paragraphs.

1. Why did your parents choose the house that you live in? Does it suit your family best?
2. Why is there so much variety in people and animal houses? Use several examples.

*Thanks to Martha Verde, Cleveland Schools, Ohio

Knowledge which is acquired under compulsion obtains no hold on the mind. -Plato.

Chapter Twelve

Figuring the Point Values and Time Frame

O ne of the things teachers struggle with most in starting to design a unit is the point value and time frame. Questions such as "how many points should an assignment be worth? How many assignments do I need students to do? How long should I give them?" are common concerns. Remember though, that these are questions teachers should be asking in any type of teaching method. Layered Curriculum makes it a little more challenging as students will not be working on the same assignments at the same time and you have multiple point assignments going on in the same class period.

In designing your first unit, begin by choosing the amount of time you want to spend on the unit (e.g.: 5 days). Next, decide how many total points you want to give the unit (e.g.: 100 points). If you divide the total points by the number of days that will give you an idea of how many points per day students may work towards (100 points ÷ 5 = 20 points/day). This gives you a rough starting point for assigning points to individual assignments.

If you are going to give a brief lecture each day worth 5 points, that leaves 15 points for student work. If the work time is one hour, then a one hour assignment should be worth 15 points. A 20 minute assignment would be worth 5 points, and so on. This is now the general rule of thumb you will use for the unit. Remember, your first unit may not look as pretty as you envision - be prepared to revise, especially on this point/time issue. But you have to start somewhere.

If you have any experience as a classroom teacher, then you probably can estimate how long particular assignments take. If I want to offer a 60 minute video with notes, that would be worth 15 points. If I assign a short worksheet which should take about 20 minutes, that would be worth 5 points. A 30 minute computer program with a short quiz at the end would be worth 10 points. And on it goes.

Using this rule of thumb you can begin to design your first unit. Start writing down a list of objectives for the unit. Then for each objective, design two or three assignment choices for visual learners, two or three assignment choices for auditory learners, and five or six assignment choices for tactile learners. You'll notice right away that many of your assignments accommodate more than one type of learner. For example, videos accommodate visual and auditory learners. Computer programs accommodate tactile and visual learners.

Now go back and add some assignment choices for the other types of learners you have. If appropriate, add at least one assignment choice for students speaking English as a second language. Add some reading assignments for students with a low reading ability. Remember, poor readers are still readers, and we want to give them opportunities to build self-efficacy on reading assignments. Try very low reading level material or assisted reading with listening centers and audio-tapes. Many publishers will also provide Spanish translations on tape for some textbooks. Inquire.

Add a couple assignments which will be a stretch for your high ability students. Unfortunately, when trying to differentiate instruction, many teachers forget the high-ability and gifted and talented students. All students want a challenge, regardless of their functional level. This doesn't just mean higher reading level material. Add assignments which will really challenge a student during the oral defense. Have two of them provide a debate, analyze various text versions of an incident, etc.

Your mix of assignments will reflect your unique student population. Obviously there are some things you may not need to include and others where you will need an abundance. Personalize the unit for your students this year.

Aim for 3 to 4 times as many assignments as you expect students to complete. In other words, if you expect students to complete 4 or 5 good sized assignments, then try to offer 12 - 20 assignments choices in your *C layer*. Once that is complete, build your *B layer*. Here find three or four choices for students to apply, manipulate, discover, or problem solve on issues you've given in the *C layer*. This area is easiest to design if you brainstorm with some other teachers in your department or discipline.

The *A layer* is generally easy to design. Write down a couple of topics in the unit that are currently under debate. It is especially intriguing if you can identify issues of current events. Pose the topics as questions for students to answer. If you are stumped on *A layer* questions, ask colleagues. I find the best suggestions often come from teachers completely outside of my discipline or grade level. Use the newspaper or news magazines for ideas currently being discussed and debated on the topic. Samples of *A layer* questions can be found in the workbook.

There it is, your first unit. Ready to go. Remember, don't be disappointed if it doesn't flow quite as you planned. Layered Curriculum may take some time to evolve into a workable teaching method for your particular population. But once you have something that works, the rest is a snap.

Subsequent units are easy to make if you use your last unit as a template. Simply pull it up on the word processor, remove or modify activities that were not to your liking, add a few new ones, then just change the topic (remove the word "bird", replace with the word "mammal") and you're on your way.

If you're not sure on how long the unit will take, guess small rather than large. It is easier to add time to a unit when you see it's running tight rather than shrink a deadline.

Most importantly, have fun with it. If Layered Curriculum is done right, the students, teachers and parents are happy and enjoying the learning process. If any of those three parties finds it additional work, more stressful, or less beneficial, then something is not right. If that happens, back up, slow down and try again with fewer choices and tighter deadlines.

-81-

A child mis-educated is a child lost. - John F Kennedy.

Chapter Thirteen

Designing Grading Criteria, Standards and Grading Scales

Before giving out your very first Layered Curriculum unit, I strongly suggest making a grading rubric or criteria for each type of assignment you will be using. One of the big mysteries in school for students is the grading scheme. I think they really believe we just throw darts at a board sometimes.

Grades should not be a surprise. People do their best when they know what is expected. Additionally, relationship building works best when expectations are clear and communication runs both ways. And probably most important, rubrics help take the whining out of the classroom. You know the question, "How come she got 18 points for her picture and I only got 10?" There is no point in having to answer those types of questions. The solution here is clear, up-front expectations spelled out in grading rubrics or written criteria.

A grading rubric is simply your standards spelled out clearly and given ahead of time. It tells students how things will be graded and what they need to do or learn in order to get full credit for the assignment. If you offer a poster assignment worth 20 points, will all posters get 20 points? Of course not. So, what does a 20 point poster look like? A 15 point poster? A zero point poster? Not only does it help the students in the work effort, but in the end, rubrics save the teacher a lot of grading time as well. Once you know what a 10, 15, and 20 point poster looks like, grading is much easier.

What you want to do is write down the 10 or 15 basic types of assignments you may offer - book questions, videos, vocabulary, flash cards, computer work, posters, models, etc. Now establish on what basis they will be graded. For example, in my room I have this rubric for computer work:

> *The computer programs are simple programs with self-tests at the end. They are worth 10 points. I will ask you 5 things about the program and you will get 2 points for each one you get correct. You need to have worked the program for at least a half hour.*

That should be pretty clear to most students. Now they know exactly what they need to do to work the assignment and what they are expected to learn and how they will be graded.

Taking the mystery out of school will change the dynamic in your classroom. It also saves the wear and tear on your nerves from defending your grading system after the fact. I actually print these rubrics out on large pieces of paper and post them around the room. As I add new assignments during the year, I add new rubrics. The simple version (like above) remains up on the walls around the room. More detailed rubrics are given to the students at the beginning of the year with their disclosure statement. Examples of both types of rubrics are found at the end of this chapter and in the workbook.

Grading and Grade Scales

Another area of frequent dilemma is the actual grading scale. My Layered Curriculum units always last two weeks and they are always worth 100 points. (I am of a concrete sequential mind style). My grading scale looks like this:

$$86 - 100 = A$$

$$71 - 85 = B$$

$$56 - 70 = C$$

$$40 - 55 = D$$

When people first look at the grade scale I use, their first response is usually, "wow, that's a really low grade scale". And compared to many of the more traditional grade scales, it certainly is.

However, the actual numbers on my grade scale really mean nothing numerically. They are place holders. My students receive letter grades at the end of the year. In other words what shows up on their report card is an A, B, C, D, or F.

My initial plan was to design something that was easy to manage mathematically. Knowing that ultimately the points would end up represented as a letter grade, the points themselves were fairly meaningless. I was trying to get something that would work with the layers and reflect my personal expectations. So I asked myself that all important question: "What do I expect from my students in my class?" If you have never asked yourself that question, it is time. What do you expect students to do to get a passing grade? What do you expect for a C? How about a B or an A?

Personally, I thought that a student who wanted a C in my class should be coming to class everyday, participating in the lecture notes and doing 3 or 4 good sized assignments. You may have very different expectations for your class - and that's fine, but those were my expectations. So I started adding up the points. Lecture notes were worth five points and assignments generally 5 to 15 points. I put a little breathing room in there for less than perfect assignments and that's the range I set for a grade of C.

Next I had to consider how much of the B layer I expected to be mastered in order to actually get a B on the unit. Obviously I wouldn't be comfortable awarding a B to a student who completed a really awful B layer assignment worth only one or two points. So how much work, learning and mastery did I expect to be worthy of the grade? Lastly I had to set a minimum expectation for the *A layer* as well.

I played around with the mathematics a bit to make it easy to manage and be doable for the students, and viola' - my grading scale.

What is important here is that teachers can assign any number of points to assignments and change the grading scale to anything that fits their school requirements or teaching comfort. The key is to find something that works with your school setting. Whether you use numbers, letter grades or smiley faces, you can make Layered Curriculum fit.

Once you've decided how much weight or time you want students to devote to the various layers, start assigning points to the layers. There is a lot of flexibility here. Our school district may dictate that 93 - 100 is an "A", but who defines what 93 - 100 looks like? We do. It really comes down to setting your own personal expectations and sharing them with your students ahead of time.

Remind students that the different layers do not guarantee that grade. In other words, just because you complete a *B layer* assignment does not mean you have earned a *B* on the unit. They will still need to do a sufficient number of assignments in the *C layer* as well.

Term Grades

I like my grade scale and it has served me well for many years. Students can understand it and it's easy to calculate. What they and I really like is that I can calculate the term grade by putting all the points into one pot for the term grade. That way if students find themselves one or two points short of a grade on a particular unit, they can make them up on the next unit. It allows everyone to see on the first day of school where they need to be by the last unit. It accommodates students who start the year a few days late or transfer in mid term.

We complete four, 100 point units per grading term. At the end of the term then, there have been 400 points possible. Students can add up their four units, divide by four and have their grade. The 400 point term grade scales is also posted on my wall.

Grading Quarter Totals - Grade Scale

344 - 400 = A

284 - 343 = B

224 - 285 = C

160 - 233 = D

Sample Rubrics

Science through Art (Poster: 20 points)

20: poster is on sturdy poster board. The illustration is an original work showing a creative blend of several sources (listed on back). Good use of white space, border and key ideas. Demonstrates an understanding of the subject (can explain 5 things learned). Creative, colorful, and well polished.

15: Poster is on sturdy poster board. Illustration is somewhat original and based on one or more sources (list on back). Ideas may not be as clear. Demonstrates partial understanding of the subject (less than 5 things learned). May need some polish to be complete.

10: Poster reflects learning but is not an original work. Colorful but may not be on sturdy poster board. Ideas clear.

5: Poster hastily done. Few ideas expressed. Not original work. One color. Not suitable for display or does not indicate learning.

Science through Textbook Readings
(Book work: 15 points)

15: Answers are clear and written in writer's own words. The question may not be written, but is understood in the answer. Student is comfortable explaining any question and can elaborate on questions as needed.

10: Answers are written in writer's own words. Student can answer at least half but not all questions in oral quiz. Not completely confident in understanding of material.

5: Answers may not be in writer's own words. Student can answer some (less than half) of the questions in oral quiz.

Science through Writing
(Short answer assignments 10 points)

10: Writing is original and neat with few grammatical and spelling errors. Ideas are clear and the writer is comfortable explaining 3 or 4 of the ideas written. If writing is not in English, the writer has gotten written feedback on grammar and spelling from someone fluent in that language.

5: Writing is somewhat original but contains grammatical and spelling errors. Writer is comfortable explaining only 1 or 2 of the ideas written. If writing is not in English, the writer is able to translate any portion of the writing, verbally.

Science through Technology
(computer work 10 points)

10: Student has spent at least 30 minutes working through the program. Student is able to explain 5 concepts learned and can answer 2/3 questions regarding program.

5. Student has spent at least 20 minutes working through the program and can explain at least 3 concepts learned. Students answers 1/3 questions regarding program.

Science through Video (Video watching
assignments 15 points)

15: Students watched entire video, uninterrupted by other activities. Notes were taken representing entire video. Students is able to explain 5-7 ideas learned from the video and can answer 2/3 of the questions regarding it.

10: Student watched entire video, uninterrupted by other activities. Notes may be sketchy. Student can explain 3 or 4 ideas learned and can answer some (less than 2/3) questions regarding movie.

5: Student watched at least 75% of the video. Can explain 3 or 4 ideas learned but cannot answer more than one question regarding movie.

Thinking about Science
("A" layer assignments 20 points)

20: At least 3 recent (less than 5 years old) scientific-based journal articles are attached to assignment. A thorough 3 sentence summary of each article is included written in writer's own words. Video presentation is 2 to 5 minutes. Presenter is comfortable with the material, makes good eye contact with the camera. Opinions are based on the research -- either the research is mentioned in the report or ideas are clearly connected with the research.

15: At least 3 recent scientific-based journal articles are attached to assignment. A thorough 3 sentence summary of each article is included, written in writer's own words. Video presentation is 2 to 5 minutes. Presenter does not seem comfortable with the material, eye contact is lacking. Not all opinions are clearly linked to the research.

10: At least 2 recent scientific-based journal articles are attached to assignment. Sketchy summaries are included. Video may not be 2-5 long (at least 1 minute). Presenter reads material. Not all opinions are clearly linked to the research.

5: At least 2 recent scientific-based journal articles are attached to assignment. Summaries included. No video presentation of opinion

Samples of simpler rubrics posted on the classroom walls.

HOW DO I DO FLASH CARDS?

Flash cards are made with plain 8.5 x 11 paper (regular size paper). Fold it in half and in half, and in half....open it up.....you should have 8 squares. Cut along fold lines to make 8 small "cards". Use 2 or 3 pieces of paper to make enough cards for the number of vocabulary words. Write the word on one side of the card. Write the definition, in your own words on the other side of the card. Learn them. They are worth 10 points.

Grading: I will choose 10 cards at random and ask you those words. You get one point for each one you know

HOW DO I GET CREDIT FOR THE LECTURE?

Lectures are worth 5 points/day. You must be present for the entire lecture to get credit. NO EXCEPTIONS. An outline of the topic will be on the overhead and you need to copy that outline and then fill it in based on what I say during the lecture.

HOW DO I GET CREDIT FOR VIDEOS?

Videos are generally worth 15 points for each 45-60 minutes of video. To get those points you must watch and pay attention to the video during that time. 10 points is given for watching it and the other 5 come from you telling me about 5 things you've learned from it.

HOW DO I GET POINTS FOR MISC. READING IN SCIENCE.

You may read for at least 45 minutes on a Science topic in newspapers, magazines, books, etc. Please tell me before you begin what topic you are reading on. Upon completion I will ask you to tell me about your reading. Your summary is worth 10 points based on enthusiasm and information gained from the reading. You should be able to explain and defend 5 things you learned from the reading.

HOW DO I GET CREDIT FOR WORKSHEETS?

Worksheets are generally worth 5 points each and you can do up to 3 on any unit for a total of 15 points. I will ask you 3 questions about the worksheet and points are based on how you respond to the questions.

It takes a lot of courage to show your dreams to someone else. - Erma Bombeck.

Chapter Fourteen

Implementing Layered Curriculum School-wide

F or all the reasons mentioned in the previous chapters, Layered Curriculum like any other type of teaching method, should not be mandated by administration. Teachers, just like students, do not like things mandated. They want choice and choice leads to creativity. Therefore, the best way to implement any type of wide-sweeping change is through a slow process using a "seed" group.

To begin a school wide implementation, organize a small group of interested teachers to begin designing units and implementing those units in their classrooms. Make the units available through some type of in-house professional library, Intranet or website.

Ideally, you should try to get a diverse group of subjects represented, but the most important criteria is just a willingness to participate. As these pilot teachers begin to share ideas and success stories with the others in the building, the idea grows.

An excellent resource for Layered Curriculum ideas will come from your special education department. When I visit with schools around the country, one of my first suggestions is to do away with special education as a separate department and integrate it into the whole school.

These valuable people should be specialized in a particular discipline and then work as a member of that department.

I recently visited a high school with eight special ed teachers in a faculty of 85. The special ed teachers taught a variety of subjects in self-contained classes. There was little contact between special and regular education teachers. My suggestion was to disband the special ed "department" and have each of the 8 teachers be a member of a regular education department. These special consultants would then work with the regular education teachers as advisors and creative consultants to help modify and design instructional ideas. So now the English department has a special education advisor who specializes in modifying regular English classes for diverse learners. The science department has a special education advisor who helps design science classes and instructional activities. The Social Studies department has a special education advisor, as do the technical industries classes, etc. This allows a more seamless presentation of expertise and reduces the chasm which has developed in many schools.

Some schools could make better use of their special education teachers in the regular classroom. I was visiting one school where many classes were "team taught" with a regular and special educator in the room. Many of these classrooms were not using the special education teachers to their full value. Sadly in some classrooms, the special education teacher could have been confused with a parent aide. The regular ed teacher was still in control, did the direct instruction and assessment. The special educator simply monitored behavior. What a waste of a wonderful resource.

Before whole-class modifications can become a reality school-wide, the school needs to rethink the division lines between regular and special educators. First and foremost we are educators, highly trained and enthusiastic about helping children. If you erase the line between special and regular education, what you will get is extra-special education. The placement of all students in the building on a level educational playing field with opportunity and learning activities for everyone regardless of ability, disability, learning style, language, or culture.

Chapter Fifteen

Using Layered Curriculum to Increase Learning

One of the most obvious uses of Layered Curriculum is to help secondary schools implement interdisciplinary approaches to instruction, as well as provide an avenue for elementary level classrooms to build thematic units of instruction.

This book is not designed to adequately describe the advantages of interdisciplinary instruction, nor give a great detail of instruction in it, but it is an area that lends itself to Layered Curriculum.

To really understand the advantages of interdisciplinary teaching we need to examine the workings of our long-term memory. The reference and cross-reference structure of this memory system is especially enhanced through this type of teaching and learning.

Memory Systems

When we learn something, we do not learn it as an isolated free-floating factoid. We in fact learn it in the context of the setting. So, we may store the new information in a memory category based on a class we were in, who we were sitting with, the clothes we were wearing, the teacher, the weather, the emotions we were feeling or even the shoes we had on. We store things in our memories under categories titled "things I learned in Health Class", and "Things I learned while sitting next to Jill", and "things I learned from Mr. Patterson," or "things I think are disgusting."

In my workshops I point this out by asking participants to list all the categories they have in their memories for the word "dog" within a certain time limit.

You may have it under a category called "animal". That means that if I asked you to list "animals", you may start with elephant, lion, horse, cat, dog.... etc. So "dog" is found in the category of "animals." Other categories we'd find dog under might be *mammals, things with 4 legs, things that bark, things that smell when wet, words containing 3 letters, things with a tail* . . . and the list goes on and on.

That's the first step of memory storage - putting things in a broad category or two or three. The second step is that our brains will start to cross-reference these categories. So "things with a tail" is cross-referenced with "things that bark" and "things that smell when wet." Some of the cross-referencing is done automatically, and some must be shown to us. In fact, most of the fun in learning later in life is to find new relationships or cross-references of ideas we haven't noticed before.

During retrieval of information from our memories, we will frequently access words and ideas through our cross-references in addition to the original categories. The more cross-references we have, the easier it is to access and understand an idea.

Retrieval failure in memory can often be blamed on a lack of cross-references. Most of us have had a frustrating retrieval failure on something that was not firm in our memories (usually a name of some sort). Our brain will begin to access all the cross-reference categories but we are unable to find the word. We may know that it starts with a "W" or maybe "M" and is a long word, with some double letter in it. We may even know how many syllables it has and can almost see the word, but can't get to it. This sort of retrieval failure is common with words and ideas with few cross-references. Rarely would you hear someone say, "What's the name of that animal that barks, has four legs, and smells when wet." That would seem absurd since "dog" has so many references and cross-references.

Tying this back to interdisciplinary instruction then, we can see how teaching a concept in more than one class, more than one subject, more than one perspective can help students set up cross-references in their memory systems. If students learn about early American music in history class and in music class and then study the structure of the lyric in English class, they are much more likely to remember the idea. And application of the concepts is infinitely easier with such a dynamic perspective.

Getting the School Involved

The first step to interdisciplinary instruction is generally setting up a simple matrix. This is done by having teachers of various subjects list what topics are taught throughout the year and when. After this information is assembled, the matrix can be examined to look for places where some topics overlap or places where units may be joined. Many elementary teachers are familiar with this concept in building thematic units of instruction. Layered Curriculum units lend themselves nicely to this concept.

If two or three subjects would like to try to join their topics, a unit can be designed around a common theme. The teachers could build one unit which would serve all classes, or preferably, have each teacher design a unit for his or her class and have some assignment choices overlap. Again, my suggestion would be to start small and go slowly. The first unit might be jointly designed around a common theme with only a few assignment choices in common. After the first unit, the teachers will now have a better understanding and idea of how to overlap further. Even the students may be brought in on the design process.

Another school-wide approach is to simply have some assignment choices that may involve another class. For example, having students write a poem on the Native American perspective of the European invasion on a history unit, and having it reviewed by their English teacher, would be a simple way to combine courses. You may have students write a report on the health risks of smoking for their health class, but have it typed up in the word processing class. Some assignments for science may have to be done in a foreign language and read to their foreign language teacher.

With planning, teachers in both classes may offer points and a grade for the same assignment. This type of overlap does not require the same commitment as a full interdisciplinary program but may provide a good starting place for one. It certainly does help with storage into long-term memory by helping establish cross-references of information.

Accountability, Responsibility, and Critical Thinking

School Boards, communities, districts and educators are very concerned with accountability, violence, diversity and preparing students for the changing economy.

One of the big cries from communities across the country is the need for accountability. State-mandated and district-mandated tests are becoming the norm. Testing and accountability are becoming key issues in the political arena. Research supports student-centered teaching methods as a way to increase long-term retention.

Layered Curriculum is one of the easiest student-centered programs to implement, particularly at the secondary level where teaching complex content to diverse learners is a challenge. Designed by and for regular educators in real-world classrooms, Layered Curriculum works with existing teaching materials and skills. With a focus on student responsibility and accountability, Layered Curriculum is a practical solution for improving test scores.

Layered Curriculum puts the emphasis on learning, not just doing. It gives credit where credit is due and hold students very accountable for actually learning material, not just putting in the seat time.

In addition to holding students accountable for learning at every assignment, the various layers of the unit encourage more complex thinking. In order to improve their grade, students are required to elaborate and play with ideas. They are required to develop leadership skills in *A Layer* assignments which ask the really tough questions in the world. It is never too early to start kids thinking like leaders.

Improved Memory Retention

One of the first things schools notice in adopting Layered Curriculum is improvement in end-of-the-year exams. There has been an abundance of research showing that student-centered instructional methods, like Layered Curriculum, lead to better retention for end of year tests. It is difficult to teach concepts in September that students must retain until a test in May. This is especially true in teacher-centered classrooms where learning is rather passive. Layered Curriculum requires students to take an active part in the learning process. The fact that they choose assignments, gives students a feeling of ownership which translates into longer retention. The oral assessment also assures that learning takes place and that students have more cortical involvement during the learning process. Most of us know students who have managed to limp through school with passing grades but without much actual learning. These students are generally not held accountable for learning and can store enough information in the short term and do enough class and homework assignments that they can pass the course even without real understanding, long term storage or ability to apply and transfer that knowledge. These are the students who are going to struggle with end-of-year assessments. A student-centered approach holds students responsible for learning right from the beginning. Students learn how to really learn and are held highly accountable for their learning.

Educators know that memorization isn't learning. Memory involves the rote list ability of the sub-cortical hippocampus. Real learning takes place in the cortex and involves patterns and relationships. Help students understand the difference and the importance of that difference.

These days come and go, but they say nothing, and if we do not use the gifts they bring, they carry them as silently away.
--Ralph Waldo Emerson

Chapter Sixteen

Layered Curriculum and Brain Imaging Studies

In the last 10 years the amount of information coming out of the neuropsychology field has been overwhelming. Unless you have been teaching on another planet for the last few years, the term *brain-based education* has come across your desk. Although the research continues to pour in and many more years will be needed to find the best applications for education, some common themes are emerging.

Stress

First and foremost is the relationship between stress and learning. Stress can be one of the biggest obstacles in the learning process. We know that stress can have significant detrimental effects on areas of the hippocampus responsible for memory storage. We see stress affecting development of the pre-frontal cortex leading to problems with sustained attention and impulse control. We see stress early in life changing brain neurotransmitter levels, permanently, leading to low frustration tolerance and increased violence.

In addition, memory retrieval is nearly impossible under stress. Even the simplest of items cannot be retrieved from our memory when we feel under pressure or stress. Think back to your college days when you were desperately trying to retrieve something from your memory during a test. You knew you knew it, but you just simply could not find the information in your head. The harder you tried, the worse it became. And when did the information pop into your head?. . . the moment you walked out of the room!

Learning requires a low stress environment. Certainly a little bit of stress is good as it adds motivation and interest. But learning requires a strong, safe and secure relationship between the learner and the teacher. Higher level thinking and learning requires an environment safe for risk-taking because truly creative thinking requires risk. Creativity simply means doing, thinking and behaving different from the norm. People will not be creative if they feel threatened, intimidated or ineffective.

The needs of the world today require a level of creativity and problem solving higher than ever before. Survival in the information century requires that workers are no longer just cogs in the system. Workers need to think, create, problem solve and adapt quickly. These are the skills of the higher regions of our brain. Training people in these areas requires allowing practice in using higher levels of their brain. This will not happen in an environment of intimidation and control. Intimidation and control are useful in training non-thinking workers. The traditional military model served this purpose. Their needs were for soldiers who were trained to learn a task and obey orders without question. A creative soldier was not the goal. A military battlefield is not the place to stop and work out alternative strategy options with a superior. Many people feel the traditional military model would work well in school and perhaps it does if your goal is clean quiet classrooms full of obedient children who are trained not to think but simply follow orders. However, if your goal is to produce thinking, creative children well-prepared for the new world, this model will not be effective. Even the military has redesigned its traditional training methods in many areas which require higher-level thinking on the part of the soldier.

Another key concern in the education community is the apparent increase in violent behaviors in schools. Violent behaviors correlate with stress. Stress comes from the perceived lack of control over one's situation and encourages the use of more primitive regions of the brain.

Therefore, teacher-centered classrooms may actually reinforce those regions of the brain which elicit violent behavior. Teachers find that student-centered classrooms significantly reduce disruptive behaviors.

Creativity and Control

Neuroscience is making two points very clear. Number one, the brain is a use-it-or-lose-it organ. Use it and it grows and develops. Quit using it and it becomes dysfunctional and the neurons actually atrophy and die. Point number two, the brain's functional priorities are from the bottom up - from the more primitive to the advanced. The lower portions of the brain are wired for survival, the higher levels for thinking and creativity. In order to reach the higher levels, one has to satisfy the needs of the lower regions.

The lower regions of the brain are satisfied by having physical needs met, having safety needs met and having the perception of control. One of my colleagues notes that "people want to **work for leaders**, but **manage** those under them."

True enough, and the reason for this is control. We only truly feel in control when those in superior positions over us allow us the control for our own actions and those we are responsible for, do as we say. Teachers are no different. We want freedom from administration to teach as we feel best, and students who obey our every word and are never less than perfect.

But we must remember how it makes us feel when we are managed from above. How creative do you feel when you are told exactly what to teach, when to teach it and how to teach it? There is a reason that most schools do not use packaged lesson plans. Most teachers are given some freedom in instructional design. Why? Because that freedom, or perception of control leads to more creative teaching and better cooperation in the school building.

Yet, most teachers are frightened to trust that the same would be true in a classroom. How do students feel when they are told what to learn, when to learn and how to learn? Are they creative? Are they cooperative? A classroom runs much smoother when students also are given some choice in their instructional strategies. I'm certainly not advocating that everything be left up to the students. They certainly are willing to work with some guidelines, just like you are willing to work with some guidelines mandated from above. But you will se an increase in creativity and problem solving when you allow students some input in the learning process.

Circadian Rhythms

Another biological issue to consider when designing school environments to facilitate learning, is the time-of-day needs of students. Psychologists have known for years about circadian rhythm differences in humans. There are basically two groups of human circadian rhythms. One of the ways to determine your group is to look at body temperature changes throughout the day. For all of us, our body temperature is at its lowest point first thing in the morning, before we even get out of bed. In one group, that temperature stays relatively low until around 90 minutes after sunrise it starts to rise significantly. It will stay elevated for the next 12 - 14 hours. These people are called *larks*.

In the second group, the body temperature stays low in the morning for an extra hour to hour and a half before beginning its great rise. It will remain elevated for the same 12 - 14 hours. These people are called *owls*. Most of us know which group we are in. For the most part, pre and post adolescents are larks and adolescents are owls.

Typically, a person is born into the world as a lark. In their early childhood they enjoy getting up early (early morning cartoons took advantage of this) and getting to bed by 9:00 pm was no problem. Somewhere around the age of 10,11, or 12, most people magically turn into owls. (Actually its not magic, it has to due with the hormones associated with puberty). These people no longer enjoy seeing the sun come up. Noon seems a more reasonable hour to rise and staying out until the wee hours of the morning is not a problem. This clock runs usually until the early to mid 20's when once again we change back into a lark. There are all kinds of exceptions to this as many of us post-adolescent owls know.

Traditionally we have blamed these changes on social events such as leaving college and getting out into the real world. It has nothing to do with joining the real world, but more with the fact that leaving college coincided with the age when most owls changed back into a lark.

Although all this information was made available a couple of decades ago, education is still lagging behind the research in practical application. This can be seen in the start times of most junior and senior high schools. Although we know the majority of our students at this age are *owls* we start most schools at 7:30 or 8:00 in the morning.

Apparently we are not running the schools for the students, but rather for the teachers, administrators and parents. I have often heard people say that students could function at this early hour if they really wanted to and should just "try harder." Trying harder is not the issue. The problem lies in the basic biology of the adolescent. They really function better later in the day.

In recent months, the sleep deprived state of the adolescent brain has become an issue of major concern. Much research indicates that our adolescent students need between 8.5 and 10 hours of sleep every night in order to fully wire in all that was taught the previous day. A 7:30 am start time makes it nearly impossible for a 6th grader to get their required 10 hours of sleep.

Why aren't more schools looking at later start times? The most common reason is parent pressure. Parents have put pressure on schools to start earlier because the parent's day starts earlier. Longer commutes and increased time demands from employers have increased the parent work day. Parents want children out of the house before they head off for work. The traditional reason given for early secondary and later elementary start times is that most parents prefer their middle and high schoolers waiting on a bus in the dark rather than their elementary students. But in light of the new research, many districts are re-thinking this traditional schedule.

I washed me face and hands before I come, I did. -Eliza Doolittle.

Chapter Seventeen

Inclusion and At Risk Populations

D iversity in the typical classroom is overwhelming. Teachers are expected to accommodate and be sensitive to the needs of a very mixed community. Diversity can mean and involve racial, cultural, socio-economic, gender, language, ability, political, and religious issues. More than any other modern nation, the United States seeks to educate its masses. We feel a tremendous obligation to educate everyone and as fairly as possible.

Little more than a few decades ago, education in this country was focused on the white, middle class, non-disabled child. Today our communities demand equal opportunity for all. Although this is obviously a wonderful change in attitude which we all enjoy, it presents a problem to the typical classroom teacher as teaching methods and teacher education has not always kept up with the changes in the school population. While we should celebrate the wonderful success our country has had in promoting education for all, teachers feel unprepared for their increasing role in the education of children with disabilities and the increasing cultural and social diversity issues they are asked to accommodate.

Accommodation needs to be done in the least restrictive environment and without stigmatizing anyone. Layered Curriculum places all students on a level playing field while meeting the needs of a vast variety of learners.

Layered Curriculum seeks first and foremost to engage students. It does that by providing a vast array of optional learning avenues which meet the needs of a diverse population. Even students with a history of failure discover that they can learn when allowed the freedom to learn in their own style and modality. Self-efficacy and self-esteem increases and failure rates decrease.

And one of the best ways to fight the increasing incidence of adolescent depression is to build self-esteem and a sense of belonging. Schools can do this by focusing on teaching philosophies which help assure a successful learning experience for all.

Special Education Classifications

Although by no means an exhaustive list, these are the disabilities most often seen in the regular classroom.

Attention Deficit and Attention Deficit/Hyperactivity Disorder (ADD/ADHD)

A student diagnosed as ADD or ADHD has a neurological disability. It affects about 5% of the general population, or 1 in every 20 students, males are more frequently affected. When inattention includes hyperactivity, the child's diagnosis is ADHD. Many children have inattention without hyperactivity. They have ADD. There is a genetic component to ADD causing it to run in families. However, many prenatal and postnatal factors have also been linked to ADD/ADHD.

Parts of their brain, especially the frontal lobes which handle planning and attention and the Reticular Activating System in the hind brain, have a chemical imbalance which limits blood flow and functioning. This makes it difficult, even impossible, to focus attention on the important stimuli in the room (like the teacher) and ignore the unimportant stimuli (like the fan noise).

Students with ADD have been successful in school through a combination of three types of interventions: structure in their learning environment, formal behavior management programs, and the use of stimulant medication (such as Ritalin) to normalize brain function.

Autism and other Pervasive Developmental Disorders (PDD)

Students with pervasive developmental disorders, such as Autism, Rhett's and Asperger syndrome, have severe problems with social interactions and an extremely narrow field of interest and activities, making peer relationships difficult. Language and other communication skills are usually severely impaired. The majority of these persons have mental retardation, but high functioning persons are able to attend school and succeed in the in regular classrooms.

These students often have severe auditory processing problems which means they cannot process what they hear quickly enough to understand verbal instruction. This may be intensified somewhat by an unfamiliar voice so it is particularly difficult toward the beginning of the school year. These students typically do not interact much with other students, and group projects and discussions will be challenging. Any type of change is particularly difficult for students with PDD.

Communication Impairments

Students with a communication impairment have speech issues that interfere with their ability to communicate. They may have trouble formulating, expressing, receiving, or interpreting oral language. Students with receptive language deficits experience difficulty comprehending oral language such as class instructions and lectures. Students with expressive language problems may understand oral instructions but may experience difficulty retrieving words and organizing their thoughts to be understood by others.

Emotional Disturbance (ED) and/or Behavior Disorder (BD)

Students with an emotional disturbance may show inappropriate behavior and feelings. Their ability to learn may be hampered by depression or general unhappiness. They may have difficulty with interpersonal relationships and demonstrate aggression or anxiety.

These students may also appear withdrawn and are often reluctant learners. They are frequently absent or tardy. They may be confrontational and challenge authority. Students with emotional disturbances are easily frustrated and often have incomplete work.

Fetal Alcohol Syndrome

Fetal Alcohol Syndrome and Fetal Alcohol Effect shows itself in both physical and mental disabilities. In addition to nervous system problems and deficiencies in growth, persons with FAS may have facial abnormalities, and are frequently mentally retarded as well. Their attention span is short and memory systems impaired. These students need definite structure to the school day and work best within very small time constraints and meeting short-term goals. Teachers need to be consistent, brief in instruction and persistent.

Gifted and Talented (GT)

Although not a disability, giftedness is considered an exceptionality in many districts and should be taken into consideration in the regular classroom. Specific criteria for giftedness varies from school district to school district, but generally includes a combination of IQ score and academic achievement. These students generally need approaches to learning that involve organizing, processing, and managing information in a divergent manner.

Learning Disabled (LD)

A student labeled as LD, or learning disabled, has difficulty processing information. They may struggle with one or more of the following: language, memory, listening, speaking, reading, writing, spelling, math or motor skills that cannot be attributed to their intelligence level. LD is a large category of students with average or above average intelligence who fail in school. This means that IQ tests and other types of testing indicate that the student *should* be able to do some task which they are unable to do or have difficulty doing. They have a problem with storing, processing and/or producing information which is reflected in the way they receive and express information. Learning disabilities range from mild to severe.

Included in this category are students with dyslexia, dyscalculia, and dysgraphia. These students have problems with reading, math, and writing, often due to language development problems. To be categorized as learning disabled the student generally must have *at least* average intelligence, with a measurable difference between their potential and their performance in an academic area. Some may be gifted students in one or more areas. These students *can* learn, but need material presented in a different modality or form than the traditional classroom offers.

Tourette's Syndrome (TS)

Tourette's syndrome is a category of tic disorders. Unlike other types of tic disorders, Tourette's is a life-long disability. The tics accompanying this disorder may change over time in both complexity and frequency. A person with Tourette's may have both motor and vocal tics. These rapid, apparently purposeless movements may include eye blinking, facial tics, throat clearing, yelling, barking, coughing, spitting, touching themselves or others, arm flapping, obscene phrases, or stuttering.

Weeds are flowers too, once you get to know them. -Eeyore in Winnie the Pooh.

Chapter Eighteen

Frequently Asked Questions

Following are the most frequently asked questions from teachers around the globe as they work on implementing Layered Curriculum.

Do Students have to start with the *C layer*, then do the *B* and *A layer*?

Usually, but not always. For the most part, the *B layer* is designed to give students the opportunity to manipulate the information gleaned in the *C layer*. If however you are doing some "stand alone" labs

or projects in the *B layer*, you may allow students to start anywhere on the unit sheet.

Sometimes *B layer* projects are things that "run along the top" of the unit, as I call it. For example, if there is a lab which will require students to grown or sprout a seed, they may have to actually start that on the first day in order to get it finished in time. However, the lab would just require a few minutes of their class time each day for record keeping, watering, etc. So these labs are worked on a little each day of the unit -

hence the term "running along the top".

When I first started using this style of instruction, I insisted that students start at the bottom and work up. But, I discovered some logistical problems with everyone needing to use the library on the last day or two for their *A layer* assignment. So I started allowing students to work on the A layer assignment at any point in the process. In fact many students will begin with the *A layer*, then come back and start building their lower layers.

Make sure that every student sees a need to start at the lower layer too. Remember that even your brightest students do not know all there is to know on a topic and they too can add to their knowledge bank. Put some more challenging (and therefore higher point value) assignments in the *C layer* to accommodate your highest ability student.

Of course, if students start in the *B or A layer*, remind them that simply completely a *B layer* does not get them a B on the unit. Regardless of which layer a student begins with, they will still need to fill out the remainder of their points from the bottom *C layer*.

Ideally, a unit should build through the layers. Basic content in the *C layer*, application/manipulation in the *B layer* of concepts learned below, and then a critical analysis or evaluation in the *A layer*. This is the goal. However, from a practical standpoint, it may be better or even necessary to allow some work in random order. It just depends on the subject and grade level.

Can Students do More than One B or A layer assignment?

In my classes, no. In other classes, perhaps. Again it depends on how your unit is set out - triangular shaped, diamond shaped or otherwise.

In the triangular shaped model used in my biology class, I have many students ask this same question. They just want to do three library critical thinking questions and be finished. I've set Layered Curriculum up so that the bottom layer is the widest, because that is the area where students build their foundation in general knowledge. If they only did *B or A layer* assignments, they would miss out on the opportunity to collect that general level knowledge. The state assessment that my students are required to take demands a lot of general content information. So in order for them to pass the state assessment, they need that basic knowledge. From a practical standpoint, I am held accountable for teaching the minimum state core requirements. I can't do this, if students only work the middle and top layers.

Do you lecture?

Yes, I lecture everyday. However, my lectures are all offered as an optional assignment.

At the beginning of class, I put an outline on the overhead projector while students are coming in and settling down. I tell the students, "This is the topic I'll be covering today in lecture. If you are going to listen and take notes, copy down the outline. If you are not doing that assignment please work on another unit assignment quietly until we are finished."

Amazingly nearly every student in the room chooses to do the lecture assignment every single day. Had I mandated the lecture and notes, they would not be near as open and willing. It is amazing what the perception of choice and control can do. Notice by offering it as a choice, the reality of the event hasn't changed - only the perception. The reality is I'm lecturing, they're taking notes. All that has changed is their perception of who made the decision to do that.

Does your course follow a textbook?

I try not to have any course I teach center around a textbook. I like students to view textbooks as a resource - one of several places to gather information. So for that reason, I do not use a class set of any particular book. I use several textbooks. I may have 10 or 15 different ones to choose from. I try to have an assortment for different reading levels. I have college level texts, high school, even elementary level textbooks. Students can find a book at their reading level.

I will issue students a textbook if they'd like one. They may also check out any of the texts in the room. This really keeps the focus off of a textbook-driven curriculum. If there is a book assignment it may be done out of any of the books. The assignment might read "Find and read the chapter on Plant Reproduction from a textbook. Be prepared to answer the end of the chapter questions." Sometimes I will specify a particular textbook to use for an assignment, sometimes not.

The assignments out of the lower level texts would not have the point value associated with them that the higher level textbooks do. This is especially true if there are specific book assignments or publisher generated worksheets which go with a specific book. Students could do several at a lower reading level to equal the tougher assignments at the higher level.

The same variety issue holds true with magazines and periodicals. I use a variety such as *Scientific American, USA Today, National Geographic*, even *Ranger Rick*. There is something for every reading ability.

How is your classroom set up?

My classroom looks fairly traditional. I do have resource and material centers set up around the room. There are lab tables and other student desks in the middle. I have a small TV/VCR unit set up in one corner, a couple of computers in another area. Magazines and newspapers are set on a table in the front. In the back is our art supply area. This area has paper, glue, scissors, old texts and magazines to cut from, markers, crayons and string. A large bookcase houses most of the textbooks. An overhead projector is at the front.

Students do not need to work in a specific area (except for the videos and computer work). They can get their materials and come back to a table to work. I allow a five minute period between lecture notes and work time so that students can get their materials, books, video, etc. and get started.

With so much going on at one time, how do you monitor for destructive behavior?

This is a great question. My class is extremely student-centered. That means that students take responsibility for their learning. They have control over the assignments, pace and direction. Once control is shifted in a classroom from teacher to student, it is amazing how behaviors change as well.

Many years ago, I worked at a zoo in Oklahoma. One of my jobs was to tour elementary school students through the zoo when they came for field trips. Frequently, while touring the Pachyderm building on days when the elephants were chained up indoors, we would experience a rather embarrassing situation. The elephants would pick up their own dung with their trunks, wait for the building to fill with children, and then hurl the dung at the students.

This behavior was hard to explain because it does not occur (from what anyone can tell) in the wild. Zoo people call it "captive behavior". Other behaviors that fit into this category were the behaviors in the primate building where you would see the gorillas and other primates eating what you and I would consider quite disgusting material from the cage floor, or birds who were bald because they pulled out all their feathers. Anytime zoo people see behaviors in animals in zoos that are not seen in the wild, the catch-all phrase of "captive behavior" was used.

I include this story, because I firmly believe that much of what we teachers see in the school classroom is "captive behavior." Destructive and disruptive behaviors frequently occur when students feel captive and in situations with little or no control. Once students are given control, these behaviors tend to disappear.

Students want to learn and be successful when put in a situation in which they feel creative. When the teacher mandates assignments such as, "we're all going to read the chapter on Abraham Lincoln today" the student who doesn't enjoy learning through reading, or is a poor reader, may find his or her own way of being creative with the chapter on Abraham Lincoln. Those are the situations that cause Abe to have his teeth blackened out, or creative additions to the story inserted by students. Give students a choice, and not only are they not destructive, they are in fact, quite protective of, proud and invested in their assignment. Nearly all students are engaged in some task all the time. This too, reduces those "captive behaviors".

I won't tell you that all behavior problems completely disappear and you will never have another frustrating moment. There are no magic wands. However, a student-centered approach will greatly reduce your behavior problems. Some do continue to crop up now and then and you have to resort to your basic teacher skills to deal with them one-on-one.

In my classes, if I'm having a problem with a particular student, I generally choose a textbook assignment for him or her, take the student and the book work to another science class, and let them work in there for the day. (We have that arrangement in our department) At the end of that time, we discuss options and see if they'd like to return to class.

So most of your day is spent walking around your room?

Yes. Except for the 15 - 20 minutes of lecture, the rest of the period I walk around the room. I make sure everyone is working, help students find interesting and appropriate assignments, orally assess their *C layer* assignments, and help organize materials. My school uses a block schedule so class periods are 80 minutes long. I can get around to all students at least twice each period, sometimes three times.

Even in my very large classes of 33-40 students, I can still get around to everyone twice. If you teach on the more traditional 45 or 50 minute period, you can still get around your classroom at least once, but usually only on non-lecture days.

Try to view your position as more of a facilitator or coach. Teaching and assessment are individualized. Make a personal contact with each child every day. This is your time to monitor behavior, progress and learning and encourage and direct young minds.

Do you have formal tests or other grades?

Most teachers still use a formal written evaluation at the end of each unit or every two units. However, the use and frequency of tests varies widely and is another area of Layered Curriculum that is open to teacher preference.

In my general biology classes, the unit sheets have become the entire basis for grades. This gives complete control for both learning and grades to the student. I feel very strongly that the oral defense is a better assessment tool than my old paper and pencil tests I used years ago. I get a much better feel for what my students are learning and I can correct errors in thinking immediately. The students also understand that the oral assessment is a trade off for not having formal exams. Occasionally I will offer a reading quiz as an option in the unit.

Layered Curriculum takes the mystery out of school and shifts the responsibility for learning from the teacher to the student, where it belongs. Students have complete control over their assignments and grades and are accountable for every class and homework assignment they do. On the first day of the term the students know how many points they need to accumulate during the term for the grade they want. Once students understand this concept, they love it - and parents too.

If tests or other activities (such as class starter quizzes or attendance) will be factored into the student's grade, make sure they are listed on the unit sheet as well. You want the student to be very clear on how their grade is determined.

Does this model work in all disciplines?

Great question, and one of the most frequently asked. Layered Curriculum works in all subject areas and with all grade levels. I originally designed Layered Curriculum for my high school biology classes. I was not happy with the number of failures nor the level of student involvement and retention. After I'd worked out the method in my classroom I saw a huge increase in student involvement and a reduction of failures. Eventually colleagues were asking how they might modify the method for their subjects. After some discussion, we found ways they could use this in their classes as well.

Soon the idea started spreading around the school and around my district. As teachers began making units, we could see a real need for a way to share the units with other teachers, so the **help4teachers.com** website went up. Originally a host for secondary lesson plans, the call started coming for elementary and college ideas as well, and so the website continued to evolve. Today the site hosts hundreds of Layered Curriculum units sheets in grades from kindergarten to college and in nearly every subject you can think of. Contributions come in from teachers around the globe. The creativity on the part of teachers is impressive.

English and Social Studies teachers have apparently found it extremely useful as the majority of the unit sheets we get come from those fields, especially middle school. However numerous examples are available in music, health, PE, math, art, foreign language, science, marketing, word processing. The list goes on and on.

Teachers use it for lower elementary, upper elementary and all the secondary subjects. Some sample unit sheets are found later in this book. Others are continually added to the website and are there as a free exchange among educators.

Every teacher finds ways in which it needs to be modified to suit their teaching style, their particular population and their subject and grade level. Remember, all you really need is:

- Choice
- Require more complex thinking to improve the grade
- Increase accountability on the day to day assignments.

What do you do with students who finish early?

It doesn't happen too often as my units are structured so that it takes even my brightest students working all five days to complete the unit. One thing I do to help students pace themselves is I will not grade more than two *C layer* assignments on any given day. This prevents them from saving them all up and bringing them in on day five. If they do that, they'll have to choose their favorite two assignments to be graded.

Once in awhile, I will get a student who has completed the entire unit with an hour or so to spare. These are generally very bright students who don't create too many problems. I first give them the option of working on school work from another class. If they don't have something else to work on, I use them as aides and pre-graders. They may pre-grade or assist with flash card assignments or listen to magazine summaries. Sometimes I'll give them an article I'm going to use on the next unit and let them make a worksheet for it. Most students love to help in this way. Under no circumstances are students allowed to just sit and do nothing in my room. I have a policy that my classroom is not a student lounge. If you are in the classroom, you must be working and learning.

What do you do with a student who loses their unit sheet?

Believe it or not, it rarely happens. As I mentioned earlier, I keep a file cabinet in my room for student use. Each period has their own drawer. I encourage the students to keep their work, including their unit sheets in the room. However, there is a back-up plan.

As I discuss assignments with students I write the points received on the top of the assignment itself, as well as on the unit sheet. I keep all these assignments in a box. All the notes, bookwork, flash cards, worksheets, etc. go in the box. Art work such as mobiles, posters, and models are displayed. If a students should happen to lose his or her unit sheet sometime during the unit, they simply have to come in after school, pick up a new unit sheet and rummage through the box to find all their assignments so that we can put the unit back together. Generally, once this option is mentioned, they go home and find their lost unit sheet. I have had a few students who have actually lost their sheet and it's not that much of a problem for them. As I said, though, it is a rare occurrence.

Do some students still Fail?

Unfortunately, yes. It is still possible to fail, although you have to work at it really hard. Layered Curriculum was originally designed as a teaching method to reduce failures. And in that, it has succeeded. If students come to class and participate, they will generally pass. The biggest reason for failures is lack of attendance. I have some students, who for various reasons, come so sporadically that they simply cannot accumulate enough points.

As I have always worked with "at-risk" populations, I have put a high priority on student engagement. It is important to get students working. If a student is doing nothing, then the unit sheet is failing, not the student. Sometimes you have to visit individually with the child to find out what interests her and what type of assignment modification you may need to help get her started. The key is to have something for everyone.

I have found students do "nothing" for two reasons. Either they cannot or think they cannot do the assignments, or they are here for a power struggle with the teacher. When Layered Curriculum is done right, both of these issues take care of themselves.

Can a student get a D?

Yes. Even though I refer to a "C", "B", and "A" layers, it is possible to get a "D". On my grading scale, 40- 55 points on any unit is a "D". So if the student only accumulated points in that range, they'd have a "D" on the unit. Chapter Thirteen discusses the grade scale and grading system in much detail.

What about homework. Should it be optional?

Teachers have handled homework with Layered Curriculum in a numbers of ways. In my classes, homework would simply be part of the unit. If students work quickly and have an efficient use of their class time, then all work could be completed in class without homework. If they work slowly, or absent, then some of the assignments may be done at home.

In fact, I always include activities that can be done from home. These could be things like finding and watching a documentary on television pertaining to the unit, looking for newspaper articles, and other sources of current events, or family field trips. Not only does this help involve parents in school work, it provides an option for students who are absent due to extended illness.

Some teachers have specific assigned activities that must be done as homework. These can either be included on the main unit sheet or given as a separate assignment. I know of a few schools, where only the homework is done as a Layered Curriculum unit. The class time is spent on whole-class instruction.

You may find it easiest to do *C layer* assignments during class time and leave *B layer* or *A layer* assignments for homework. While it is possible in my classroom to do the whole unit during class time if you really use your time wisely, most students find they don't want to work that diligently. Most of them take their *A layer* assignment home to do over the week-end. Again, this is an issue that can be modified to fit your individual needs or school requirements.

Chapter Nineteen

Tips, Hints and Suggestions

L ayered Curriculum has been used in hundreds of classrooms with a wide variety of grades, populations, subject matter and teaching styles. The real beauty of Layered Curriculum is in its flexibility. It is wide open to elaboration and modification. As the model has been used, here are some of the logistical tips and strategies that have been found to be helpful in implementation.

Tips:

~**Color code the unit sheets**. My classes do four units per quarter, eight per semester, 16 per year. Each is copied on a different color. It's much easier to just refer to the "green unit" or the "red unit". At the end of a grading quarter, they can quickly pull out their "yellow, green, red and blue" sheets, add them up, and they have their grade. This helps all of us stay organized.

~Worried about students losing their unit sheet? On the first day of school, **give every student a file folder**. Have a file cabinet in the room with a drawer for each period. Allow students to leave their materials in the room if they need to.

~**Keep a bucket of extra pencils and pens**. I pick up spares in the halls or on my floor and throw them in the bucket. We all want students to come prepared, but some students struggle with the simplest of organizational skills and we can help them most by not making a big deal out of it.

~**Check out the policies of your local Public Broadcasting television station** for using taped programs in your classroom. Most have policies giving schools re-broadcast rights for at least a year. Some of the educational daily programs make excellent video options for units. You may find that some of the programing has a teacher guide available.

~**The daily newspaper can be brought in each day.** Many cities offer the newspaper for free to teachers and schools (paid for by vacation newspapers in the community). Let students find articles pertaining to the unit.

~**Display and hang as much student work as possible**. When students know that their work is going to be displayed, they invest more effort. Also investigate hanging or displaying some in the hall outside your room. Although most elementary schools fill the hall with student work, this tradition gets lost in secondary schools.

~**Post grading rubrics everywhere.** It may help to color code the rubrics as well. Then when a student asks about how to do an assignment, you can just refer him to the pink sheet on the back wall.

Hints:

~As students finish C layer assignments, **sign them off right on their unit sheets**. I simply initial the assignment and put the point value next to it. If you'd like a back-up, you may also put the points earned on the actual assignment before putting it away. This helps if there is a dispute, or a student has to reassemble her unit sheet because the "dog ate it."

~Putting the points in the margins of the unit sheet will also give students a visual reminder of what they've done. If you put a grading scale and due date on the units as well, students get a visual of
1. How far they've come.
2. Where they want to go.
3. When they need to be there.

~When starting this teaching methodology, **go slow.** Design and try one unit and see how it goes. Keep notes and modify for the next unit. The first one is the hardest. One you have a workable plan, it's just a matter of cut and paste on your word processor.

~Also remember to **go with your comfort level.** If your teaching style does not allow as much student choice as mine, then don't offer so much. Layered Curriculum can be done in dozens of modified ways. Perhaps you are more comfortable giving whole class instruction for the entire *C layer*. If so, then maybe you could allow some student choice in the application and critical thinking levels.

~If you have students who are proficient in a foreign language, have them **translate a couple of unit sheets into their native language.** This makes a good resource if you have new students transfer in who read little or no English. It is nice to have something in their own language to get them started. It won't be the same unit everyone else is working on, but at least you have something to get them engaged with. Assignments on this would have to be done with illustrations or some other non-language based form.

~**Use the last 5 minutes for clean-up.** I sometimes offer job choices for an extra five points per unit. Students can sign up to do a clean-up job each of the days for a particular unit. Jobs might include: organizing textbooks, organizing art supplies, clean up t.v. area, shut down computers, trash, making sure desks and chairs are put back. When everyone leaves and the dust settles, you can easily see who has done their job. This is especially helpful if you teach a wide variety of subjects and have to start fresh with the next class.

Learning Style Suggestions:

For Visual Learners

~**Supplement your lectures** with visuals. In addition to just notes on the board or transparencies, try to use models, charts and other visual aides. Even when offering a taped lecture or reading, set out visual props for students to look at or manipulate during their listening time.

~Provide all students with a **written copy** of assignments.

~Whenever possible, **write a backup** on the board for any verbal instruction or direction.

~Allow **written reports** as an alternative to oral ones.

~Provide a **written copy of board work** for those who may need it. For example, if the vocabulary words are written on the board, it may be helpful to some to have a few photocopies of the words made. Many students get lost/distracted in copying from the board to the paper and back again.

~When discussing abstract concepts use **visual representations** or allow students to use or make manipulative objects.

~**Use visuals** like bulletin boards, posters, transparencies and graphs. However, be careful with a visually busy classroom. Some students are overwhelmed and distracted with too much visual information. You may want to a have a visually quiet area of the room as well.

~In addition to textbooks, have students **read other things** such as newspapers, bulletin boards, maps, magazines, brochures, or labels.

For Auditory Learners

~Record assignment directions on tape so students can access them as needed. Some students have extremely poor reading skills, so although they can sound the words out in reading the assignment, they have no comprehension. It helps if you take the first day of a unit and read the entire thing out loud.

I've also found that I get a lot of "takers" if I **offer to read magazine articles**. Magazine articles are a favorite assignment choice of my students, but many struggle with reading. So I may say, "I'm going to read the Chicken Pox article aloud in that back corner. If anyone would like to come and listen, they are welcome." I'm amazed at the turn-out.

~Have a variety of textbooks available for different reading levels. Textbook salespeople are a great resource for this. When they ask if they can send you a sample copy of a particular book, always accept. You can get a huge assortment of reading material this way. Also, be sure to inquire as to whether or not a Spanish audio version of a textbook is available. More and more publishers are offering it.

~Tape record certain textbook chapters. You can sit in the comfort and quiet of your home on a Sunday afternoon and read a chapter into a tape recorder. You may want to simplify the vocabulary when possible. The assignment is for the students to read along while listening to you read through headphones. At the end they can come to you and have their oral defense. When I tried this I was so very surprised at how many students choose the assignment. I now offer it frequently.

~Give oral and written quizzes. Offer them as options. Some students like to take publisher printed quizzes that come straight from a reading assignment.

~Offer a variety of ways for students to verbalize ideas. Try class presentations, small group presentation, oral reports, discussion groups, debates, and panels.

For Tactile Learners

~**Have manipulative objects** for abstract ideas. Better yet, have students build the manipulative objects themselves.

~**Keep a table of art and craft supplies** in the room. Include string, scissors, play-doh, construction paper, markers, baggies, etc. Allow students to use a variety of materials in creating models.

~**Have students measure properties** such as temperature, weight, size and distance. This is especially fun if the object is very large. Also, have them make scaled drawings or representations of large objects.

~**Dioramas are still fun**, no matter what grade you teach. Remember, they are those displays, models and representations put in a shoe box or other small box.

~**Mobiles, out of various materials,** are simple and great options for tactile learners.

~**Have students construct a board game** teaching a certain number of concepts. To pass it off, they must play it in a group.

~**Drawings, charts and graphs** are excellent activities. You may occasionally want them presented on something other than on plain paper. Try 3-D graphs or having them display them on a bulletin board.

~**Have students build models, maps, bulletin boards.**

Chapter Twenty

Sample Unit Sheets

H ere are some sample units of Layered Curriculum designed by teachers around the globe in various disciplines and grade levels. Additional sample units can be viewed at the website, http://help4teachers.com

General Biology DNA & Protein Synthesis

Section I C Layer   Maximum 65 points.
1. Listen to the lecture and take notes each day. (5 pts/day)
   1   2   3   4   5
2. Flash cards on vocabulary terms. 10 pts.
3. Write a paragraph on Watson & Crick's discovery of the structure of DNA. Must be done in a language other than English. 10 pts.
4. Read a chapter on DNA. Answer 5 questions (you choose questions = 10 points. My choice = 15 points).
5. Design a creature using characteristics on board. Write DNA sequence for him. 10 pts.
6. Find 2 newspaper articles from 1953-54 on the discovery of DNA structure. Copy and paste them on paper. Highlight important features. 15 pts.
7. Read Gene Therapy article. Answer questions. 10 pts.
8. Read Wheat article. Give an oral summary 10 pts.
9. Watch the video on DNA. Take notes and give me an oral summary. 10 pts.
10. Work the computer program on cells. 10 pts
11. Using the color code on the board, color a DNA sequence for your creature in #5. 10pts
12. Using the DNA sequence for your creature, write the mRNA, draw the tRNA and the amino acid sequence. 10 pts.
13. Work two worksheets on protein synthesis. 10 pts.
14. Find a current (this year) magazine or newspaper article on a gene discovery. Give a summary. 10 pts.

Section II B Layer Labs Choose only one 15 pts.
1. Bring in a container. Plant a seed. Chart it's growth for 2 weeks. What is it's average growth per day?
2. How do veins vary in flies? Use at least 4 different flies and a microscope.
3. How do thumb lengths vary in human adult males? (Use at least 20 subjects).

Section III A Layer. Choose only one. Use an "A- layer sheet" 20 pts
1. DNA fingerprinting. Has it helped court cases?
2. Is genetic engineering in crops a good or bad thing?
3. Will the human genome project be finished on time?

Grades: 40-55 = D   56- 70 = C   71- 85 = B   86+ = A

_____   _____
parent signature/date   contact phone#
(sig. & phone worth 5 points in C layer)

Here's a short mini-lesson.

Intro to Life Science, Biochemistry, & Cells.

Section I C layer Maximum 65 points.
1. Listen to the lecture and take notes each day. 1 2 3 (5 points/day)
10 point assignments:
2. Flashcards on vocabulary terms.
3. Build a 3-D cell with a plastic sandwich bag. Include 12 organelles
4. Read a chapter on cells and answer 6 book questions.
5. Make a 3-D poster of two types of cells.
6. Find a newspaper article on nutrition. Give an oral summary.
7. Work the computer program on cells.

Section II B layer Labs Choose only one
1. Can you get a seed to sprout using only water? How long will the plant live?
2. How do heart rates vary among animals? Use 3 different animals.
3. What happens to a leaf if covered in foil for 2 days? 5 days?

Section III A layer. Choose only one. Use and "A- layer sheet"
1. Exercise, Good or Bad?
2. Athletic shoes, Good or Bad?
3. Vitamin supplements, Good or Bad?
4. Dieting, Good or Bad?

Grades: 40-55 = D 56- 70 = C 71- 85 = B 86+ = A

Astronomy - Earth/Moon Unit II*

100 points possible: A is 90 points B is 80 points C is 70 points D is 60 points. The student should be prepared to orally defend each project.

C Layer 79 points maximum
1. Watch the two movies "Apollo 13" and list 10 things that were different and 10 that were the same. 20 points.
2. Draw the magnetic field of the earth and of the moon. 10 points.
3. Draw a picture of the movement of plate tectonics. 10 points.
4. List 5 things that are different in how Aristotle viewed the moon as compared to how we view the moon today. 10 points.
5. Make a table of 5 characteristics comparing the earth and moon (i.e. diameter, orbit, info, etc.) 10 points.
6. Draw the earth and moon to scale on the same piece of paper. 10 pts.
7. Observe, draw, and label the phases of the moon for 4 days. 10 pts.
8. Find 10 questions about the earth and moon and answer them. 10 pts.
9. Flash cards for 10 vocabulary words including at least 4 describing the phases of the moon. 10 points.
10. Describe 5 things (processes, observations, etc.) Which shows how the surface of the earth is different than the surface of the moon. 10 pts.
11. In a language other than English, describe the difference between waxing and waning. 10 points.
12. Take a quiz on day #3 from your notes. 10 points.

B Layer 10 points maximum
1. Draw, label, and understand the phases of the moon over a 2 week period.
2. Describe in detail how we can know the time by looking at the moon.

A Layer 10 points maximum
Write a paper (200-400 words) using at least 3 references on one of the following issues. Take a stand and state your opinion.

1. Should we continue exploration of the moon?
2. Is there any value to the exploration of other planets and stars to those of us on earth?

*Created by and used with the permission of S. Gene Van Tassell, Granger High School, Salt Lake City, Utah.

Dr Martin Luther King Jr.-- 5th-6th grade

Objectives:

- Identify African-Americans and their contributions to American Society.
- Describe what African Americans did and explain how it positively changed our way of life.
- Increase children's self-esteem, making them more likely to be tolerant of others and respect others' rights.

Basic Level: All activities must be completed in this level before you proceed to the next level.

(Choose Number 1 or 2)
1. Listen to lecture and take notes on Black History.
2. Listen to lecture on tape and respond to questions.

(Choose one of the following 3)
3. Define given vocabulary words
4. Make a crossword puzzle using the vocabulary words
5. Make flashcards with the vocabulary words.

(Choose 6 or 7)
6. Take an online quiz to see what you already know about Martin Luther King Jr. Go to this website
http://www.educationplanet.com/redirect?url=http://www.seattletimes.com/mlk/classroom/MLKquiz.html
7. Go to the website below and do the Scavenger Hunt.
(http://www.educationworld.com/a_lesson/hunt/images/sh_ws_mlk.)

(Everyone will do number 8 on the 3rd class day)
8. Participate in Pre-Video discussion, watch video, "Separate But Equal", and complete question sheet

(Working with your group Choose 4 of the remaining activities to complete)
9. Using the following website respond to the situations presented. For each situation discuss with your group what the correct response would be. http://www.landmarkcases.org/brown/equal_same.html
10. Participate in Class Collage Activity (Activity Attached)

11. Create a poster-Look At Me. (Activity Attached)
12. Create a Black History Quilt (Activity Attached)
13. If you moved to a new school, how would you want people to treat you?
14. Participate in the Role Model Activity. (Activity Attached)
15. Read Poem "Martin Luther King Jr." and answer questions (Poem attached to the end of this Layered Curriculum.
16. Make a timeline showing events that happened in Dr. King's life or another famous African American using dates and pictures. The following website can assist you with the timeline. www.enchantedlearning.com

Mastery Level
Everyone must do numbers 1 &2. Choose two between 3& 6.
1. Everyone needs to be cared for by someone - this is a right we all have. What happens when people don't get enough attention? Write a story about a time when you felt lonely, isolated or hurt by the way someone treated you.
2. Plan to Perform a "Random Act of Kindness". Write a paragraph that describes what you plan to do and why.
3. Write and perform a commercial that sends the message of equality.
4. Write an essay explaining the changes Martin Luther King Jr. made during his lifetime that continue to affect us today. Include and explain what you can do to help Dr. King's dream of peace become a reality.
5. Write a "I Have A Dream Speech". Include in the speech your own personal Dreams.
6. Read the document you were given on "Declarations on the Rights of a Child (http://www.unhchr.ch/html/menu3/b/25.htm). Reflect on three of the Principles of this document. How would you change them? Write one principle that you think should be added to these principles for today.

Advanced Level (Choose One)
1. Research and write an essay giving reasons why Black History Month should continue to be celebrated.
2. Write a Letter to the Governor of your state. Tell them what you think needs to be done to make our state and world a better place for all people regardless of their creed or color.

*Designed by Marilyn Washington, St. Amant, Louisiana

KEYBOARDING - 7th Grade
Unit 2: Finger Group Lessons 11-20

Name _____ Due Date _____

70 - 77 = D   78 - 85 = C   86 - 92 = B   93+ = A
You must orally defend what you have learned from each of the
following assignments: Note:
 Activities worth 5 points should take about 15 minutes.

C Layer (No more than 85 points):
1. (Required-70 pts) Participate fully in daily dictation lesson (3.5
pts/day).
   11 12 13 14 15 16 17 18 19 20
AND Key each line once in the corresponding worksheet (3.5
pts/worksheet)
       11-1 12-1 13-1 14-1 15-1 16-1 17-2 18-1 19-1 20-1
2. (5 pts each) Work 1 or 2 of the following lessons in Microtype Pro,
Section A: 8, 12, and 16.
3. (5 pts) Create a list of at least 15 words using all of the letters in this
unit. Type the words 10 times each.
4. (10 pts) Read a news article (approved by the teacher) about computer
technology and key 5 questions and answers.
5. (10 pts) Create your own drill page of 15 lines, 5 of the lines must
contain words, capitals and tabs. Exchange your drill sheet with a friend
and key the other student's drill sheet.
6. Develop an assignment of your own with teacher approval. (Points
determined by teacher)

B Layer: Choose one - 7 points (You must earn a minimum of 5 points
to get credit. Assignments used in previous units will not be duplicated.)

7. Create a game that reviews and evaluates all of the alphabetic keys.
8. Type an approved assignment for another class. (at least two pages,
double spaced, size 12 font)
9. Design and key a children's book. Illustrations may be hand drawn but
words must be keyed.
10. Retype an approved Dr. Seuss book.
11. Develop an assignment of your own with teacher approval.

A Layer: Choose one - 8 points (You must earn a minimum of 5 points to get credit. Questions used in previous units will not be duplicated.) See my web site for more instructions and the A-Layer Template (lc020.k12.sd.us)

12. How might keyboarding skills enhance your career opportunities?
13. Do you think computers enhance student creativity?
14. Do you think computers have improved education?
15. Develop a topic of your own with teacher approval.

Note: All keyed assignments must contain a header and must be corrected and evaluated before being turned in.

* Designed by Lorrie Cook, South Dakota

Psychology 1010 - College Freshman

Mon. Evening
If you miss a class, besides being responsible for getting the lecture notes, you will need to make up the points through additional assignments. Some of these may be done in class, others at home.
There will be a 100 point exam at the end of this unit, so the following count toward 1/3 of your unit grade.

Unit one. Appendix A: Statistics & Chapter 2 Biological Psychology
Due _____ Name_____50 points possible.
All labs need Question, Hypothesis, Procedure, Data and Conclusion.

1. Is there a relationship between shoe size and g.p.a.? Use 25 subjects. 15 pts.
2. Video: The human brain.(Write 10 interesting things) sign roll at the end. 10 pts.
3. What is the average (X) STM? Use 20 subjects. 15 pts.
4. What does the current research say about Alzheimer's? (Summarize 3 pieces of research, write a paragraph summary of each. List Title, publication, date, author). 15 pts.
5. Research new and old technology in brain imaging. Include CAT, PET, EEG, MEG. Write a good paragraph on each. 10 pts.
6. Group discussion: Is there as much prejudice today as when Martin Luther King made his famous I had a Dream speech? What has changed? What has stayed the same? Discuss this topic within a group of 3 - 5 for approximately 20 minutes. Have a facilitator to keep the discussion moving, a recorder to jot down key points and ideas, and a writer to write a final summary (approx. one page). Write down the names of the people in your group and their role. 15 points.
7. Listen to Lecture and take notes (sign up by 7:00 pm to get credit). 5 points/ night

Date_____ Date _____ Date_____

Here's an example where the *C layer* is broken into specific days for students who want more structure. They still need to find time during the 5 day unit to work on the *B and A layer*.

Mammals
Section One C Layer 65 POINTS MAX
Day 1
1. Take notes from lecture 5 pts.
2. Make 15 flashcards from Terms on Board. Learn them. 10 pts.
3. Write a one page overview on the Class of Mammals. List 2 sources. 10pts.
4. Make a color picture representing various types of Mammals. 5 pts.

Day 2
Choose an Order of Mammals _____. (no duplicates/class)
1. Read and summarize 3 articles from Ranger Rick on your Order. 10 pts
2. Write 1 page overview of your Order. list 2 sources. 10 pts.
3. Make a color picture representing various members of your Order. 5 pts.
4. Watch the laser disk on your Order. Write 15 new things about its members. 10 pts
5. Make 10 flash cards of Scientific/Common Names of members of your Order. 10 pts

Day 3
Choose a Family within your Mammal Order. _____.
1. Read the section in Holt on mammals. Be prepared to answer the review ques. 10pt.
2. Write a 1 page overview of your Family. List 2 sources 10 pts.
3. Make a color picture representing various members of your Family. 5 pts.
4. List 15 animals who are members of your Family. 5 pts.

Day 4
1. Choose a specific species of mammal. _____.
2. Write a page report on their habitat. 5 pts
3. Write a page report on their reproduction/child rearing. 5 pts.
4. Write a page on environmental concerns regarding your animal. 5 pts.
5. Make a color picture showing your species in its habitat. 5pts.

Day 5
1. Watch the video. List 15 mammals found. 5 pts
2. List the scientific name of 5 of the mammals. 5 pts.
3. List the Order of 10 mammals found in the video. 5 pts.
4. Give a 2 minute (max) oral report on the Order/Family/ or Species from this unit. 10 ptst

Section Two B Layer 15 POINTS MAX - Choose one only
1. What type of Mammal was eaten by a barn Owl? Dissect a pellet and reconstruct the skeleton.
2. How is a bat skeleton similar to a whale skeleton? Draw each and compare/contrast them.

Section Three A Layer 20 POINTS MAX - Choose one only
Find 3 recent magazine articles on the topic. List and summarize EACH article and write a paragraph of your opinion.
1. How did nearly all the marsupials end up in Australia?
2. What can be done to save the Manatee?
3. Besides humans, what is the most intelligent mammal?

Grades: 86+ A 71+ B 56+ C 40+ D

General Biology Viruses

Name_____ Period_____ Due Date_____

Section I   C Later   Maximum 65 points.
1. Listen to the lecture and take notes each day. (5 pts/day) 1 2 3 4 5
2. Flashcards on vocabulary terms. 10 pts.
3. Write a paragraph on the discovery of the polio vaccine. Must be done in a language other than English. 10 pts.
4. Read a chapter on viruses. Answer 5 questions (you choose questions = 10 points. My choice = 15 points).
5. Design 4 viruses attacking 4 different cells. Include RNA and DNA structure. 10pts.
6. Find 2 newspaper articles from the 1950's or 60's explaining new vaccines. Paste them on paper. Highlight important features. 15 pts.
7. Read one of the xeroxed articles_____. Give an oral summary 10 pts.
8. .Read one of the xeroxed articles_____. Give an oral summary 10 pts
9. Watch the Virus video. Take notes & give me an oral summary. 10 pts.
10. Write a children's book about Sue, the lysogenic virus and Tom, the lytic virus.10 pts.
11. Work two worksheets. 10 pts.
12. Find a current (this year) magazine or newspaper article on an oncogene discovery. Give a summary. 10 pts.

Section II   B Layer Labs Choose only one 15 pts.
1. Interview someone with a lytic virus. Get a 3 day account of symptoms (objective and subjective). Hypothesize about what stage the virus is in each day.
2. Interview someone who has had cancer or lived with someone with cancer. Find out how the virus progresses, treatments and how the disease affected the person and family.
3. Design an experiment for testing a new AIDS vaccine. Include number of trials, subjects, and length of study.

Section III A layer. Choose only one. Use an A layer sheet" 20 pts
1. Will we have a vaccine for AIDS in your lifetime?
2. Is the chicken pox vaccine a good idea?
3. Why is Utah last in the nation for vaccinating our children?

Grades:
40-55 = D   56- 70 = C   71- 85 = B   86+ = A

_____   _____
parent signature/date   contact phone#
(sig. & phone worth 5 points in "C" level)

I have a dream that one day this nation will rise up and live out the true meaning of its creed: We hold these truths to be self-evident, that all men are created equal. -Dr Martin Luther King.

Appendices

Appendix A:

General Teaching Tips

If you are working with students **preparing for Advanced Placement** and other tests of that type - insist they are tested in your classroom. Cue-triggered recall is a major memory asset. Students are put at a disadvantage when tested in an environment foreign to the one they were in while learning.

Too many **students quitting at the *C layer*** in your Layered Curriculum units? Make sure your *B Layer* activities are enticing. Try assignments that involve food, live animals, or other atypical class activities. The *B Layer* choices should pull your students into that layer.

Thank your students every day, individually, for coming. Too often, students go from the beginning of the school day to the end without anyone recognizing the fact that they got up, dressed, and came to school. For many children, just getting to our classroom was a remarkable accomplishment.

Remember, **testing material** falls into the category of "unassisted reading material" and therefore should be written AT LEAST two full grade levels BELOW a student's level of reading. This is different than a textbook reading level. If a textbook is written at an "8th grade reading level" this means that 50% of 8th graders can comprehend it with teacher assistance. Obviously you don't want to use this level for unassisted exam material.

When making *A Layer* **assignments for younger children** (or even older children) have them use people rather than library research material for their references. They can get opinions on their topic from 3 different adults (or 3 different 5th graders or 3 different teachers, etc.). Have them summarize the 3 opinions, either orally or on paper, and then form their own opinion.

Have students who write well in a foreign language **translate units sheets** for you. You can keep these in a file to use throughout the year when you get new students who struggle with English but speak/read a different language. It allows them to be engaged in a learning activity right away.

Layered Curriculum works particularly well in **summer school** programs where you may have condensed time-frames for course objectives. Offering a variety of assignment choices gives students more freedom and the perception of control which encourages more out-of -class learning and work.

Those **"nature sounds" CD's** that are available everywhere make nice noise monitors in the room. Turn it down low and it tends to calm students and the noise level. In my room it helps monitor the noise level as well because when students get too loud, I just say, "hey, I can't hear the birds" (I use the rainforest CD).

January is the **peak month for S.A.D.** - seasonal affective disorder -- depression caused by decreased melatonin levels. Generally high in the winter because melatonin is produced by sunlight. In your classroom, open the shades, or if you are in a room with no windows, use incandescent light bulbs (regular screw-in type from home) to add to the light in the room. Flourescent light does not increase melatonin levels.

Research tells us that an **effective classroom** is based on student opinion, not teacher opinion. Poll your students from time to time. A simple evaluation I frequently use poses only 3 questions: what should I keep doing?, what should I start doing?, what should I stop doing?

In **math assignments** offer both book work and worksheet problems. Many children, especially those with ADHD, struggle with book work simply because they have to transfer the problems onto their own paper. They get lost, confused, and make copy errors.

Model appropriate behavior. This is especially important in situations where you are angry and upset. You can teach all the conflict resolution curricula you want, but students learn most by watching you. Remember, you may be the only person in their life who models appropriate behavior when angry.

Use cue-triggered recall to help students study for major exams. Have them wear a special shirt or outfit while studying and then wear the same outfit during the test.

Offer your lecture time as an option - you'll probably have more students listen.

Use caution when doing fund-raisers so that you are not exploiting your students. Ask yourself: are these students raising funds for an issue they feel is important and immediate to their needs (ie: a field trip, cage for the class hamster, save the park) or are they motivated by extrinsic rewards offered by the fund raising company (pizza party for winning class, trip to Disneyland for top selling student in the district, etc.?) Too often fund raisers involve using child labor to benefit an out of state company in order to raise money for a general educational issue such as technology or books for the library. These items are the responsibility of the taxpayers, not the children. In addition to exploiting our students, these practices encourage children to work for extrinsic rewards rather than intrinsic ones.

Inservice your students on Layered Curriculum and brain biology. Take the first day to teach your students the hows and whys of your teaching methods. A simple concept, but one that will make your teaching so much easier. Once students understand why you are asking them to do something, they are much more cooperative.

Color code those unit sheets. The simplest, yet most effective way to help with organizational skills.

Spend a significant amount of time early in the year working on **building a relationship with your students.** Real learning involves risk-taking and people are more likely to take risks in an environment they trust.

Treat every child like you would like your own child treated by his/her teacher.

Make sure you include students in **setting the classroom rules**. When students show up for day one and the rules are already posted, students lose that perception of control which can lead to behavior problems.

Remember the heat factor. **The brain requires an immense amount of water** to function properly. This becomes especially important in learning and especially difficult in hot classrooms. Encourage water bottles if possible or allow water breaks frequently.

Children who have any type of **auditory processing difficulty** often have increased problems in the beginning of the year. Allow even more time after asking questions until students get used to your voice and the novel visual distractions in a new room.

Try something new. Throw out the laminated lesson plans (or at least file them) and freshen your approach to teaching. Even if it is not something you continue all year, it may give you a little boost in enthusiasm for teaching again.

Color code things in the room. Instructions, folders, period files, subjects, etc. Color is wonderful in assisting with administrative skills (for teacher and student).

The best and most beautiful things in the world cannot be seen or even touched. They must be felt with the heart.
--Helen Keller

Appendix B:

Research for Further Reading

If you still need some "hard research" to back up your efforts in implementing a student-centered program, here are some references which you may use in presenting your ideas to colleagues, administration or district personnel.

Research Supporting Student-Centered Instruction

Benware & Deci 1984. The quality of learning with an active versus passive motivational set. American Educational Research Journal, 21, 755-765.

Boggiano et al., 1993. Use of techniques promoting students' self-determination: Effects on students' analytic problem-solving skills. Motivation and Emotion, 17, 319-336.

Deci, Schwartz, et al., 1981. An instrument to assess adults' orientations toward control versus autonomy with children: Reflections on intrinsic motivation and perceived competence. Journal of Educational Psychology, 73, 642-650.

Deci & Ryan, 1987. The support of autonomy and the control of behavior. Journal of Personality and Social Psychology, 53,1024-1037.

Deci, Nezlek, & Sheinman, 1981. Characteristics of the rewarder and intrinsic motivation of the rewardee. Journal of Personality and Social Psychology, 40, 1-10.

Flink, et al, 1992. Children's achievement-related behaviors: The role of extrinsic and intrinsic motivational orientations. In A. K. Boggiano & T.S. Pittman (Eds.), Achievement and motivation: a social-developmental perspective (pp. 189-214). New York: Cambridge University Press.

Grolnick & Ryan, 1987. Autonomy in children's learning: An experimental and individual difference investigation. Journal of Personality and Social Psychology, 52,890-898.

Koestner, Ryan, Bernieri, & Holt, 1984. Setting limits on children's behavior: The differential effects of controling versus informational styles on intrinsic motivation and creativity. Journal of Personality, 52, 233-248.

Patrick, Skinner, & Connell, 1993. What motivates children's behavior and emotion? Joint effects of perceived control and autonomy in the academic domain. Journal of Personality and Social Psychology, 65, 781-791.

Reeve, 1996. The interest-enjoyment distinction in intrinsic motivation. Motivation and Emotion, 13, 83-103.

Rigby et al., 1992. Beyond the intrinsic-extrinsic dichotomy: Self-determination in motivation and learning. Motivation and Emotion, 16, 165-185.

Shapira, 1976. Expectancy determinants of intrinsically motivated behavior. Journal of Personality and Social Psychology, 34, 1235-1244.

Valleran, et al. 1997. Self-determination and persistence in a real-life setting: Toward a motivational model of high school dropout. Journal of Personality and Social Psychology, 72, 1161-1176

References

Allis S. (1996, November 4). The struggle to pay for special ed. Time, p.82-84.

Atwater, M. (1995). The multicultural science classroom. The Science Teacher,60(4), 40.

Bradford, P. (1993). The first step in learning is learning to feel good about yourself. In R. Jennings (Ed.), Fire in the eyes of youth: The humanities in American education (pp. 79-86). St. Paul, MN: Occasional Press.

Bradley, D. & West, J. (1994). Staff training for the inclusion of students with disabilities: Visions from school-based educators. Teacher Education and Special Education, 17,(2), 117-128.

CH.A.D.D. (1996). Children and adults with attention deficit disorders. Ch. A.D.D. Online! Available online at: http://www.chadd.org/.

Chiras, D. (1992). Teaching critical thinking skills in the biology & environmental science classrooms. The American Biology Teacher, 54(8), 464-468.

Collins, M. (1993). Origins. In R. Jennings (Ed.), Fire in the eyes of youth: The humanities in American education (pp. 25-37). St. Paul, MN: Occasional Press.

Dalheim, M., (Ed.). (1994). Toward inclusive classrooms. National Education Association of the United States Teacher-to-Teacher Series. Washington, DC: NEA Publications.

Darling-Hammond, L. & McLaughlin, M. (1995). Policies that support professional development in an era of reform. Phi Delta Kappan, 76(8), 597-604.

Dempster, F. (1993). Exposing our students to less should help them learn more. Phi Delta Kappan,74(6), 432-437.

DeWijk, S. (1996). Career and technology studies: Crossing the curriculum. Educational Leadership, 53,(8), 50-53.

Dunn, R. (1990). Bias over substance: A critical analysis of Kavale and Forness' report on modality-based instruction. Exceptional Children,56, 352-56.

Dunn, R., Beaudry, J., & Klavas, A. (1989). Survey of research on learning styles. Educational Leadership,46(3), 50-58.

Evers, R. & Bursuck, W. (1994). Literacy demands in secondary technical vocational education programs: Teacher interview. Career Development for Exceptional Individuals, 17,(2), 135-143.

Fuchs, L., Fuchs, D., Hamlett, C., Phillips, N., Karns, K. (1995). General educators' specialized adaptation for students with learning disabilities. Exceptional Children, 61,(5), 440-459.

Fuentes, K. & Weinberg, P. (1993). New York and the world. In R. Jennings (Ed.), Fire in the eyes of youth: The humanities in American education (pp. 1-13). St. Paul, MN: Occasional Press.

Fullan, M. (1994). Change forces: Probing the depths of educational reform. Bristol, PA: Falmer Press.

Glaser, R. (1990). The reemergence of learning theory within instructional research. American Psychologist, 45(1), 29-39.

Glynn, K., Rajendram, K. & Corbin, S. (1993). Perceptual-based student outcomes assessment process in the marketing curriculum. Journal of Education for Business, 69(1), 11-18.

Good, T., & Brophy, J. (1991). Looking in classrooms (5th ed.). New York: Harper & Row.

Harris, J. (1995). Sheltered instruction. The Science Teacher, 62, 24-27.

Guild, P. (1989). Meeting students' learning styles. Instructor, 99(8), 14-17.

Hollowood, T., Salisbury, C., Rainforth, B., Palombaro, M. (1994). Use of instructional time in classrooms serving students with and without severe disabilities. Exceptional Children, 61,(3), 242-253.

Houck, C. & Rogers, C. (1994). The special/general education integration initiative for students with specific learning disabilities: A "snapshot" of program change. Journal of Learning Disabilities,27,(7), 435-453.

Hugdahl, K. et al. (2003). Neuropsychologia, Vol 41(6), 666-675.

Inclusive Education: A series of issue papers. (1994). Illinois Coalition on School Inclusion, Springfield. (ERIC Document Reproduction Service No. ED372 525).

Janney, R., Snell, M., Beers, M., & Raynes, M. (1995). Integrating students with moderate and severe disabilities into general education classes. Exceptional Children, 61,(5), 425-439.

Katz, J. (1996, May 11). Policy on disabled is scrutinized over discipline problems, cost. Congressional Quarterly Weekly Report, p. 1295-1299.

Keegan, M. (1995). Psychological and physiological mechanisms by which discovery and didactic methods work. School Science and Mathematics, 95(1), 3-10.

Kern, L. et al. (2001). Journal of Positive Behavior Interventions, Vol 3(1), 3-10

Lewis, R. & Doorlag, D. (1995). Teaching special students in the mainstream (4th ed.). Englewood Cliffs, New Jersey: Prentice Hall.

MacAuley, D. & Johnson, G. (1993, Summer). Behaviorally disordered students in mainstream settings: A pedagogical-interactional perspective. Teacher Education Quarterly, 87-100.

Manning, M. & Lucking, R. (1990). Ability grouping: Realities and alternatives. Childhood Education, 66(4), 254-258.

Moore, C. (1993). Twelve secrets of restructured schools. Education Digest, 59(4), 23.

National Education Goals Report: Building a nation of learners. (1994). US Government Printing Office. Washington, DC.

Nunley, K. (2000). In defense of oral defense. Classroom Leadership (ASCD). February.

Nunley, K. (2003). A Student's Brain: The parent/teacher manual. Brains.org.

Putnam, J., Spiegel, A., Bruininks, R., (1995). Future directions in educational inclusion of students with disabilities: A delphi investigation. Exceptional Children, 61(6), 553- 576.

Rainforth, B. (1992). The effects of full inclusion on regular education teachers. A report to California Research Institute on the integration of Students with severe disabilities. San Francisco State University. (ERIC Document Reproduction Service No. ED365 059).

Rankin, D., Hallick, A., Ban, S., Hartley, P., Bost, C. & Uggla, N. (1994). Who's dreaming? -- A general education perspective on inclusion. Journal of the Association for Persons with Severe Handicaps,19,(3), 235-237.

Renzullli, J., Reis, S. & Smith, L. (1993). The revolving door identification model. (Available from Creative Learning Press, Inc. P.O. Box 320 Mansfield Center, CT. 06250).

Renyi, J. (1993). The arts and humanities in American education. In R. Jennings (Ed.), Fire in the eyes of youth: The humanities in American education (pp. 1-13). St. Paul, MN: Occasional Press.

Sanchez, G. (1993). This hard rock. In R. Jennings (Ed.), Fire in the eyes of youth: The humanities in American education (pp. 105-113). St. Paul, MN: Occasional Press.

Schneider, Roth, Ennemaser. J. of Ed Psych 2000 vol 92,(2) 284-295.

Schrag, J. & Burnette, J. (1994). Inclusive schools. Research Roundup,10,(2). A publication of the National Association of Elementary School Principals.

Schultz, J. (1994). Inclusion: The debate continues. Instructor, 104,(4), 55-56.

Schultz, J. & Carpenter, C. (1995). Mainstreaming Exceptional Students: A guide for classroom teachers. (4th ed.). Boston: Allyn & Bacon.

Schumm, J. & Vaughn, S. (1995). Getting ready for inclusion: Is the stage set? Learning Disabilities Research and Practice, 10,(3), 169-179.

Seal, K. (1993). Performance-based tests. Omni, 16(3), 66.

Shaywitz, S. (2003). Biological Psychiatry. Vol 54(1), 25-33.

Smith, S. (1993). Enabling the learning disabled. Instructor,103,(1), 88-91.

Sperling, D. (1993). What's worth an "A"? Setting standards together. Educational Leadership, 50(2) 73-75.

Stickgold, R., et. al. 2000. Nature Neuroscience, Vol 3(12) 1237-1238.

Tindal, G., Rebar, M., Noet, V. & McCollum, S. (1995). Understanding instructional outcome options for students with special needs in content classes. <u>Learning Disabilities Research & Practice,</u>10(2), 72-84.

US Department of Education. (1991). Thirteenth annual report to Congress on the Implementation of the Individuals with Disabilities Education Act. Washington, DC: U.S. Government Printing Office.

Vann, A. (1993). Let's get the curriculum reform train off the bell-curve track. <u>Education Digest,</u> 59(1), 32.

VanTassel-Baska, J. (1988). Developing scope and sequence in curricula. <u>Gifted Child Today,</u>11(4), 58-61.

Vaughn, S., and others. (1994). Teachers' view of inclusion. Paper presented at the Annual Meeting of the American Educational Research Association. New Orleans, LA, April 4-8, 1994. (ERIC Document Reproduction Service No. ED 370 928).

Weaver, R. L. (1990). Separate is not equal. <u>Principal,</u> 69(5), 40-42.

Wigle, S. and Others. (1994). Full inclusion of exceptional students: Three perspectives. Paper presented at the annual meeting of the Mid-Western Educational Research Association. Chicago, IL, October 12-15, 1994. (ERIC Document Reproduction Service No. ED 377 635).

Willis, S. (1995, Summer). Reinventing science education. <u>Curriculum Update</u> (Supplement to <u>Education Update</u>) Association for Supervision and Curriculum Development.

Wilson, S., Peterson, P., Ball, D. & Cohen, D. (1996). Learning by all. <u>Phi Delta Kappan,</u> 77(7), 468-476.

Wlodkowski, R. & Ginsberg, M. (1995). A framework for culturally responsive teaching. <u>Educational Leadership,</u> 53(1), 17-21.

Yasutake, D., Lerner, J., Ward, M. (1994). The need for teachers to receive training for working with students with attention deficit disorder. <u>B.C. Journal of Special Education,</u> 18(1), 81-84.

Yatvin, J. (1995). Flawed assumptions. <u>Phi Delta Kappan,</u> 76(6), 482-484.

Personally I'm always ready to learn, although I do not always like being taught. -Winston Churchill.

Index

Layered Curriculum is a trademark created and owned by
Kathie F. Nunley, EdD.
Inquire for usage information.
kathie@brains.org

Additional books, guides and workbooks
ORDER FORM
3 Ways To Order:
1. Go to: http://Help4Teachers.com/books.htm
2. Fax this form to 208-979-0678 (check website for current pricing)
3. Mail this form (check website for current pricing) to:

Help4Teachers
54 Ponemah Road
Amherst NH 03031

___Layered Curriculum: The practical solution for teachers with more than one student in their classroom. $_____

___Layered Curriculum: WORKBOOK $_____

___A Student's Brain: The parent/teacher manual $_____

U.S. shipping/handling $2.50 1ˢᵗ book ($1.25 each additional book)

Total # books:_____ Total amount including shipping $_____

Visa/Mastercard #_____exp.date_____

Name on Card:_____

(in case of problems) daytime phone(_____)_____

Shipping address:_____

_____

_____

_____